Welcome to SA

Welcome! Welcome to the world of SACRED FEET Yoga and The SACRED FEET Publishing Imprint headquartered at Slate Branch Ashram in the soft, rolling hills of south central Kentucky.

Gratitude is due to the good people who took the time to send Salutations to SACRED FEET upon the occasion of our first edition. May you prosper and be happy in all your endeavors.

Thank you as well to all who have played a part in bringing The SACRED FEET Publishing Imprint into existence. May your lives be filled with contentment and steady wisdom.

We look forward to serving and participating in the vibrancy of Interfaith/Interspiritual/Intra-Tantric dialogue. May the Shakti of SACRED FEET be ever strong and pure.

Jaya Jaya Amrita Guru. Jaya Shri Jagadguru Namah.

--Swami Shraddhananda Saraswati
aka Rev. Dr. Sonya Jones, OUnI
Publisher, The SACRED FEET Publishing Imprint
Spiritual Director, Slate Branch Ashram

SACRED FEET Publishing Imprint Mission Statement

The SACRED FEET Publishing Imprint of Slate Branch Ashram is committed to the continuing development and refinement of the discipline of Interfaith Studies and Reflection. As such, SACRED FEET is devoted to bringing high quality Interfaith, Interspiritual, and Intra-Tantric manuscripts into print and appropriate digital formats. Manuscripts must analyze ideas or experiences from two or more religious and/or indigenous spiritual traditions in comparison or intersection with each other and must reflect intellectual as well as spiritual knowledge. SACRED FEET takes as its logo the Guru's *padukas*, or sacred sandals, a symbol indicating that subjects covered in submitted manuscripts must be handled with care and respect. However, manuscripts need not reflect the views of the publisher or editor. Electronic manuscripts with cover letters describing both the project under consideration as well as the author's spiritual journey and intellectual credentials are preferred.

Please contact: Swami Shraddhananda, Saraswati Order of Monastics, aka Rev. Dr. Sonya Jones, Order of Universal Interfaith, Publisher, or Sandra Simon Mangham, Managing Editor, at sacredfeetyoga@gmail.com.

Salutations to SACRED FEET

"Congratulations on Swami Shraddhananda's endorsement by Wholistika. It is good to see *Jesus Was a Shaktipat Guru* coming around to fruition as a course and teaching. It is gratifying to see SACRED FEET and Swami Shraddhananda reach wider audiences."

--Rev. Allen Brimer
Pastor, First Presbyterian Church, Somerset, Kentucky

"Well wishes from the Kingdom of Shambhala. SACRED FEET—I love the name—has a beautiful mission and mission statement regarding its work. Many thanks to Swami Shraddhananda for the work she is doing, channeling good energy into spiritual endeavors that will help wide ranging numbers of people. Congratulations!"

--Dr. Judith Broadus
Director of Societal Health and Well-Being
Shambhala Buddhist Meditation Center (Lexington, Kentucky)

"As The SACRED FEET Publishing Imprint launches, I wish for it to become a vehicle for books and authors that are, at times, ignored by publishers whose sole motivation is profit, and in so doing, become an institution that serves the new emerging world in which spiritual and moral values serve as guides. I hope that SACRED FEET will pay special attention to the spiritual needs of the young who find themselves offered many dreams with few ways of achieving them. It is my ultimate wish that The SACRED FEET Publishing Imprint will touch many hearts, opening them to wisdom, and inspiring all of us to live more authentic lives in the service of compassion, justice, and beauty."

--Adam Bucko
Spiritual Activist and Co-Author (with Matthew Fox), *Occupy Spirituality*
Co-Founder, The Reciprocity Foundation

"As President of The Jones Educational Foundation, Inc., I wish to congratulate the Rev. Dr. Sonya Jones, aka Swami Shraddhananda, for launching The SACRED FEET Publishing Imprint. This significant venture expands the mission of Slate Branch Ashram and has great potential for promoting and advancing Interfaith and Interspiritual ideas and concepts both regionally and internationally."

--Dr. Wanda L. Dodson
Professor Emerita, School of Human Sciences,
Mississippi State University

"Blessings on the important venture of SACRED FEET Publishing. The world needs a voice for authentic, deep and discerning spirituality that crosses boundaries."

--Philip Goldberg
Founder, Spiritual Wellness and Healing Associates (SWAHA)
Author, *American Veda*

"A sign of our times—as spirituality 'goes global' in this dawning age of Interspirituality—are books that place the revered founders of the world's major Axial religions in the context of the inevitably emerging global, universal spirituality. Sw. Shraddhananda aka Dr. Jones's book on Jesus to inaugurate SACRED FEET profoundly locates him within the global legacy—the birthright of emergent Awakening shared by us all."

--Dr. Kurt Johnson
Co-founder (with Bro. Wayne Teasdale), *The Interspiritual Multiplex*
Winner, A "Best Spiritual Book of 2013" for *The Coming Interspiritual Age*

"God's richest blessings on this wonderful new work: The SACRED FEET Publishing Imprint. 'Behold, make all things new,' says God through Isaiah. Thank you so much for your efforts, Sw. Shraddhananda."

--Rev. Dr. Joyce Liechenstein
Associate Director, One Spirit Learning Alliance
Secretary General, Order of Universal Interfaith (OUnI)
Wisdom Keeper, Mystical Christianity, CMH
Huston Smith Award for Lifetime Achievement

"The Council of Interfaith Communities and its co-founder, The Order of Universal Interfaith, acknowledge The SACRED FEET Publishing Imprint as a very welcome addition to our movement. The heart of Interfaith and Interspirituality begins with understanding. The SACRED FEET Publishing Imprint will grow the understanding between faith paths to new levels of revelation and knowledge. The Interfaith-Interspiritual-Integral movement offers its heartfelt thanks to SACRED FEET for stepping up to this important task."

--Rev. Tim Miner, OUnI M.Div., M.A., CBC
Executive Director, The Council of Interfaith Communities-USA
Co-founding Secretary, Order of Universal Interfaith

"May Lord Ganesha remove all obstacles and the blessings of Goddess Saraswati fill you, Sw. Shraddhananda, with inspiration, wisdom and abundance for the launch of this much needed initiative to spread the precious wisdom teachings. *Om Shanti.*

--Swami Omkarananda
Director, Sivananda Yoga Vedanta Center, Los Angeles, CA

"I offer my prayers and blessings for the launch and growth of The SACRED FEET Publishing Imprint. May it spread light and peace to all it reaches."

--Swami Ramananda
President, Integral Yoga Institute, San Francisco, CA

"Blessings and best wishes for this auspicious project. The world desperately needs a publishing house dedicated to the intersection of Interfaith, Interspiritual, Integral, and Intra-Tantric perspectives."

--Rev. Dr. Bob Salt
Founding Chair, Council of Interfaith Communities, USA
Professor & Department Chair, Human Development & Family Studies
University of Wisconsin-Stout

"Congratulations on the launching of The SACRED FEET Publishing Imprint. In this contentious modern world, it is important to hear from writers who bring together various traditions in the healing spirit of Interfaith dialogue. I know the publisher, Swami Shraddhananda, Rev. Dr. Sonya Jones, very well and can attest to the high quality of her work toward the greater good of all. Swami Shraddhananda gave an excellent talk in the Shiva Symposium at my ashram in Australia, and we enjoyed having her Personal Assistant, Sandra Simon Mangham, now Managing Editor of SACRED FEET, in residence as well. Swami Shraddhananda's seva as Spiritual Director of Slate Branch Ashram creates splendid opportunities for Interfaith learning while serving as a boon to the lineage of Bhagawan Nityananda of Kanhangad and Ganeshpuri. SACRED FEET will be a welcome addition to the contemporary spiritual landscape. I send abundant good wishes for the success of this worthy spiritual endeavor."

--Mahamandaleshwar Swami Shankarananda
Shiva Yoga Ashram, Mt. Eliza, Australia
Author, *Consciousness Is Everything*

"As an author, rabbi, and seeker of wisdom within the rich and expansive field of Interfaith Studies, I wish this new effort by Slate Branch Ashram well. SACRED FEET promises to be an important and perhaps even transformative vehicle for sharing the wisdom of the world's religions in ways that deepen our understanding of one another and the One in whom we live, and move, and have our being."

--Rabbi Rami Shapiro
Author, *Perennial Wisdom for the Spiritually Independent*

"Swami Shraddhananda's SACRED FEET Publishing Imprint is groundbreaking work and will provide a different path for readers and students to expand and deepen their personal spiritual practice and Interfaith approach. Swami Shraddhananda has been an example to me and to her colleagues at The New Seminary with her commitment to her spiritual path and adherence to the higher values that guide her. I along with the entire New Seminary community wish Swami Shraddhananda well in bringing her SACRED FEET message to a broader audience. "

--Rev. Jay B. Speights
Executive Director, The New Seminary
Author, *7 Days with Adam*

"Yeshua would be most honored to be called a Shaktipat Guru as in the title of Swami Shraddhananda's inaugural edition from The SACRED FEET Publishing Imprint. He is, through us, a leader of the Interfaith, Interspiritual movement. He led a life of love, and we can spread his teaching of love as we honor and respect all paths."

--Fr. Giles Spoonhour
Co-Founder, The New Seminary
Huston Smith Award for Lifetime Achievement

"What a gift! May SACRED FEET find the treasures buried at the heart of the deepest wisdom traditions and lift them into the hands of this beautiful, broken world."

--Mirabai Starr
Interspiritual Author, Teacher, and Translator:
God of Love: A Guide to the Heart of Judaism, Christianity, and Islam;
Mother of God Similar to Fire (With William Hart McNichols);
Saint Francis of Assisi: Brother of Creation (With Richard Rohr)

"All good graces and blessings for the launch of The SACRED FEET Publishing Imprint. Its time has come. I look forward to all the forthcoming publications."

--Rev. Philip Waldrop
Board Chair, A World Alliance of Interfaith Clergy

"Congratulations, Sw. Shraddhananda, on launching SACRED FEET! Interfaith understanding is such a crucial need in our world. I wish you all the best and send blessings for this important work."

--Cindy Wigglesworth
President and Founder, Deep Change
Author, *SQ21: The Twenty-One Skills of Spiritual Intelligence*

Jesus Was a Shaktipat Guru

Swami Shraddhananda
aka Rev. Dr. Sonya Jones, OUnI

SACRED FEET

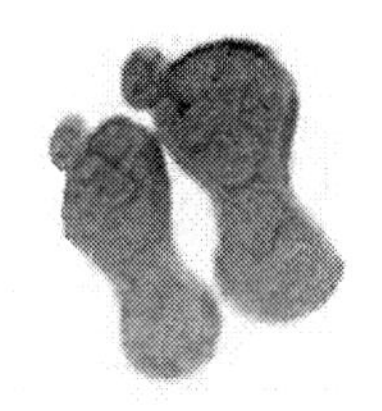

The Interfaith/Interspiritual/Intra-Tantric
Publishing Imprint of Slate Branch Ashram
The Jones Educational Foundation, Inc. (JEFI)
www.jonesfoundation.net

Published by SACRED FEET
The Interfaith/Interspiritual/Intra-Tantric
Publishing Imprint of Slate Branch Ashram
The Jones Educational Foundation, Inc. (JEFI)
P.O. Box 289, Somerset, KY 42502, USA

PHOTO CREDITS
Sw. Shraddhananda: Melissa Reid
Slate Branch Ashram: Sandra Simon Mangham

Printed in the United States of America
First published 2014

Inaugural Edition of The SACRED FEET Publishing Imprint
Sandra Simon Mangham, Managing Editor

ISBN: 978-0-9915010-1-4

For all those who have had the courage
to follow a Jagadguru
to completion

Acknowledgements

Foremost, I wish to thank my Siddha Gurus and Guides across spiritual traditions. I am indebted to my teachers in Shambhala Buddhism and to my colleagues at The New Seminary in New York City. I am grateful to spiritual seekers at Slate Branch Ashram and to students in the Honors Program at the University of Kentucky who have inspired me to think in expansive ways about the issues examined in this text. Thanks to Jenny Watkins for her close reading of an early draft of *Jesus Was a Shaktipat Guru.* To Rev. Allen Brimer, Pastor of First Presbyterian Church in Somerset, I owe a debt of gratitude for his deep knowledge of the Judeo-Christian tradition. Thank you as well to Kirit and Emma Basu, co-founders of Wholistika, for the spark of inspiration that produced a final draft of *Jesus Was a Shaktipat Guru.* Without Sandra Simon Mangham, my Personal Assistant as well as Managing Editor of SACRED FEET, The Interfaith Publishing Imprint of Slate Branch Ashram, this effort could have been far more difficult. Thank you, Sandy, dear Chamatkara, for your intelligence and your organizational skills. Many thanks are due to my UK Honors Program students in the Happiness Seminar for their final proofreading of the text. Finally, eternal gratitude is due to the Holy Spirit or Maha Kundalini Shakti for experiences which have enriched my understanding of related scriptures and commentaries across spiritual traditions.

Jaya Jaya Amrita Guru. Jaya Shri Jagadguru Namah.
(Praises to the Jagadguru Who Delivers the Divine Nectar.)

Contents

Introduction

Had *Jesus Was a Shaktipat Guru* come into my hands at the beginning of my spiritual journey, my experiences would have been validated immediately, and I would have saved myself a lot of pointless worry. Alas, I was kept in the dark!

During my childhood and teen years, I had an intense devotion to the Divine, carefully nurtured by my Roman Catholic upbringing. My yearning to know God ran like an undercurrent through everything during that period, broken only by the wilderness of adult life at university, and the gradual realisation that my hunger could not be satisfied merely by belief and liturgy.

Something in me knew there was more, but it was unfathomable. Unsupported, I turned my face away from the teachings as I understood them and put myself into suspension, living in the shadows of spirit. That, more or less, is the experience of many.

Then, one day in November 1980, something extraordinary happened that shattered all my concepts of the world. I experienced an act of grace, a sacred blessing so immense that to speak of it, even today, puts me right back into the energy and wonder of the experience.

Having placed my head upon a pillow one night, I felt a mighty current roaring through my being, filling me with an exquisite elixir of light and bliss. It poured through my hands, feet and head, totally transfixing me with golden light. I became acutely aware of my breath. On the in-breath appeared the sweet, living face of Jesus, his eyes gazing on me lovingly and with compassion. On the out-breath, my consciousness zoomed out to view the Cosmic

Christ standing in a wheel of blue light. This oscillating experience continued to play in my being throughout the night, leaving me in a state so blissful that for several weeks my children, my family, and even the pavements twinkled with blue light.

This experience, I later learned, and the ones that followed, were a form of spiritual transmission called Shaktipat, which literally means "the descent of grace." That night something momentous had opened up in me, and I was in a state of shock. One thing was certain: I needed guidance.

It is so true that once the inner light is awakened in you, it guides you to the people from whom you need to learn. I prayed to Jesus, asking to be put in touch with a living spiritual teacher, and with little effort, knowing absolutely nothing about such things, I came to the feet of Swami Muktananda and Gurumayi Chidvilasananda, Shaktipat Gurus of the Siddha Yoga lineage. Through the guidance of my beloved teachers and mentors who have followed afterwards, I have received everything I need to fulfill my spiritual journey. What a joy that is, and how immensely grateful I am!

Thirty years have passed; my path has unfolded and come full circle. I now serve in my community as an Independent Catholic priest.

You might ask, "How is this possible? That is a Hindu tradition you studied with Gurus, and you are a Christian?" This is the sort of question I have encountered more than once, and my response to those who ask is this: when we are earnestly seeking the Truth, then it is revealed, and Shaktipat is the means through which we come to experience Presence, the Divine within. Yogis, Christians, and spiritual seekers alike, no matter what our tradition, or what label we give to our teacher, all yearn to find the Kingdom of Heaven within. It is our birthright to recognise and revel in the Kingdom of One-ness. And, this process of coming to know the Kingdom within is at the heart of *Jesus Was a Shaktipat Guru.* Its words will resonate with the truth in you.

Swami Shraddhananda aka the Rev. Dr. Sonya Jones draws together many aspects of the subject of Shaktipat. She examines the background of Jesus's own training and enlightenment. She explores the context and mission of Jesus the Christ and discusses the inner meaning of his teachings. She delineates his role as a Shaktipat teacher, describes how a Guru works with his or her students, and reflects on how modern spiritual teachers are deeply connected and supported by their own "enlivened" lineages. Swami Shraddhananda aka Rev. Dr. Jones's analyses and reflections are helpful to Christians with a background of mainstream teachings, many of whom may not realise that this transmission also continues powerfully through the form of Apostolic Succession via Ordination and through the administering of the Sacraments.

Do read these pages. Everyone can learn much. These pages are the fruit of Swami Shraddhananda's own journey and many years of training working inside a living Shaktipat lineage. Her wisdom and insight come from her own deeply contemplated meditation experiences and extensive scholarship. *Jesus Was a Shaktipat Guru* is a book to be treasured, contemplated, and revisited over and over again.

--The Right Reverend Christine Vasumati Deefholts
Bishop and Ordained Priest of the Jurisdiction,
Mission Episcopate of Saints Francis and Clare,
Oxford, The United Kingdom

CHAPTER I

Jagadguru: Larger than Jesus or Buddha

Christianity started with Christ.

So says the *Encyclopedia of World Religions*. For most people, this common sense claim needs little proof. Christianity began when Jesus took issue with Jewish law as the be-all, end-all of religious truth just as Buddhism was named for its founder. Jesus is to Judaism what the Buddha is to Hinduism. Both Jesus and the Buddha are Jagadgurus, or Master Teachers, who infused their existing traditions with new life.

With regard to origins, however, another point of view deserves some thought. Just as the Kabbalah, the mystical dimension of Judaism, may have been with us since the beginning of time, so the spirit of Christ, or Christ consciousness, likely existed before Jesus of Nazareth was born.

A passage from the *Holy Bible* underscores the timelessness of Jesus the Christ. In the seventeenth chapter of John, Jesus prayed, " . . . and now, O Father, glorify me together with yourself, with the glory which I had with you before the world was."

Since Jesus was a Jagadguru or the equivalent of a Buddha, then Christ stands for the purified consciousness of a Master Teacher, or a "son of the Holy Spirit," as "The Secret Book of James" would have it, in any tradition. In all probability, Christ appeared on earth many times before the man called Jesus was born. Judging from the number of Gurus, Rinpoches, and Lamas who have graced the planet in modern times, Christ most likely has come back to earth repeatedly following the era when the historical Jesus was crucified and resurrected.

Mainstream Christians tend to read the resurrection as the enlivened body of Jesus rising from the dead and ascending into Heaven to sit at the right hand of God the Father. While a literal reading of the resurrection has theological merit, it also offers hope for the faithful to live again after death. Interestingly, resurrection placed Jesus in a position to be reincarnated back onto earth—perhaps as himself, perhaps in a different body far removed from Jerusalem. The resurrection itself also can be interpreted as the immediate reincarnation of Jesus after his death on the cross.

The idea of reincarnation is distinctly Indian in origin and far older than the Christian tradition. Certain scholars believe, however, that reincarnation may have found its way into the religion that became Christianity as a consequence of the so-called "missing years" when Jesus may have been in India or Tibet.

According to I.M. Oderberg in his article entitled, "Reincarnation as Taught by Early Christians," reincarnation circulated among early Christians during the first centuries following the death of Jesus when his disciples imparted knowledge about the pre-existence of souls and their reimbodiment. Reincarnation as such dropped out of Christian currency as the church moved forward in time, but remnants can be found in the *Holy Bible* in Colossians 2:12, John 3:3, Revelations 1:11-20, 17:8-18, and II Thessalonians, 2:1-3.

Perhaps the best known of these passages, John 3:3 is usually taken to mean that Christians must be "born again" and experience a transformation in order to be saved. While this reading is not inconsistent with the major claim of my text—that the awakening of the Holy Spirit is that which sets us free—it can also be interpreted to mean that we all must be "born again," or reincarnated until such time as the Holy Spirit completes his purifying work.

Jesus was fond of using literary devices such as parables, images, and metaphors—a tendency that has given rise to Religion and Literature as an interdisciplinary course of study. Here, in John 3:3, he may have employed a *double entendre*, or double meaning, to suggest that his followers could experience immediate transformation through grace (so rare in Indian spirituality it is said to happen every 1,000 years), or be born into the next life for a new opportunity to realize liberation by continuing the work of the previous lifetime.

When Christian scriptures and commentaries are read solely as proof of Jesus's return in a human body, certain details and dimensions risk being lost. In Matthew 17:12-15, for instance, Jesus taught his disciples about John the Baptist as a reincarnation of Elijah (also Elias or Eliyahu). Later, in the third century common era, Synesius, Bishop of Ptolemais, prayed assiduously that his soul might merge into the light, and be returned no more into the illusion of earth.

In John 14:3, Jesus said he was going to prepare a place for his disciples, and he would come again to receive them unto himself, so where he was, they might be also. His followers had to be "born again" to be received unto, or into, Jesus.

In October of 2009, a personal experience justified for me the truth of Jesus's words and the Christian promise. I came home from a long day of teaching in the Honors Program at the University of Kentucky to find my mother, a lifelong Christian, slumped in her chair. Apparently, she had suffered a stroke.

Quickly, I phoned 911. The ambulance seemed to

be taking too long to get to Mother's house. I called 911 again.

"Lady," the 911 operator said, "it's only been six minutes since you called the first time."

Six minutes? I thought. In a situation like this, one minute can mean the difference between life and death.

I kept talking to Mother, trying to keep her from floating off into the zone from which stroke victims seem not to return. She was not responding to my voice, or to my touch on her face.

The 10 minutes or so it took for the ambulance to arrive felt like 10 years. At one point, just before the drivers lifted her body onto a stretcher, Mother opened her eyes for the last time in her remarkably good and steady life. She looked me in the eye and spoke my initials, "SLJ." I took some solace in her gesture. Mother knew her only daughter was with her, and she was not alone.

The drivers would not allow me to ride in the ambulance with my best friend, so I followed along afterwards. When I arrived at the Emergency Room, Mother seemed to be resting comfortably, but she sent a signal. She batted away a tube as if to say what I already knew: "Don't let them hook me up to these artificial gizmos. Let me die naturally."

When the ER doctor entered Mother's room, he said she had experienced a massive stroke. More than likely, he added, she would not live through the night. I was not surprised, for Mother had insinuated several times in recent days that she did not expect to live into her 90s as her parents had done.

One day, she pulled out a pink tablecloth I had never seen and placed it on the round wooden table in her kitchen. "This belonged to your grandmother," she said. It was not her words that struck me as unforgettably as the strange look in her eyes. It was as if she knew something she was not yet prepared to reveal. After her death, when our cousins from Ohio came to the memorial service and stayed with me in our home, I discovered that the tablecloth had matching cloth napkins. Mother had starched, ironed, and placed them on the serving table as if she wanted me to be ready for family.

A spiritually significant guest appeared in Mother's hospital room about 3 a.m. of the morning following her stroke. As I was sitting beside her bed in the Intensive Care Unit, I heard the words, "I am going to take her to Heaven and return her as a saint." The words were faint at first, and then, I saw the figure of Jesus the Christ standing beside me.

It soon became clear: Mother would not recover from the stroke. Mother and I had talked. I knew only too well—the responsibility was mine to give the okay to pull the tubes.

Mother's friends came to pay their last respects. They could hardly believe this was happening. The week before her stroke, Mother was very active. She attended the annual Board of Trustees meeting of The Jones Educational Foundation, which she and I had established following Dad's death in 2005. She went to a friend's anniversary celebration, and together, we attended a dinner at another friend's home for one of Mother's former students who had been diagnosed with cancer. We acted as greeters in the narthex of First United Methodist Church where we also had served as lay readers to light the Advent candles.

To be 85 years old, Mother looked great. She had taught for 44 consecutive years in the county and city school systems, retiring only when it was time to care for her mother, also a teacher. Young male students could not help falling in love with Elva Sears Jones, it was sometimes said jokingly. Young women admired her and sought to emulate her ways. She was as lovely on the outside as she was on the inside.

In the year following Dad's death in April of 2005, Mother read the *Holy Bible* all the way through from cover to cover. Every night before bed, she read at least one chapter by the light of a small bedside lamp. Mother was tolerant and supportive of the Interfaith activities we hosted at Slate Branch Retreat House, but she made one point clear. Jesus was her "main man," to use her words.

At precisely 11 a.m. on the morning of October 15, the breathing machine was turned off. The senior minister of First Methodist stood quietly in the back of the hospital room to offer his prayers and support. I was leaning over Mother's bed, holding her hand, taking her last breaths with her just as she had breathed me into the world from the womb of her small body. I whispered mantras, sacred syllables, my version of prayer, to help with her release—*Om Namah Christaya, Om Namah Christaya Om.*

At 11:03, I became aware of a large angel in the room. I could feel the vibrations of a powerful set of wings just behind Mother's bed. Boom. Boom. Boom. A kind of sonic boom. The beating of the angel's wings still resonate in my being as I attempt to recollect the sequence of what happened next.

At 11:05, Jesus the Christ appeared over Mother's bed. He arrived swiftly, much like a comet. Hovering over her sweet body, he sucked her up unto himself. Her breathing stopped. Jesus was gone just as quickly as he had arrived, carrying the spirit of his newest angel in his bosom. He flew away at what seemed to me to be the speed of light.

Now, I don't know for certain, but I could venture a guess as to Elva Jones being on good terms with the Holy Spirit. To be given such a royal ride into the astral dimensions known in Christianity as the mansions, or rooms, of Paradise speaks volumes about her spiritual attainment. In addition to speaking of Mother's devotion to Christ, I referred to her as a "natural Buddhist" in my eulogy for her Celebration of Life ceremony held in the crowded chapel of First United Methodist Church. Mother was totally at peace while still in her body. The Holy Spirit seems to have finished his purifying work. Mother was a living embodiment of *santosha*, translated from the Sanskrit as deep contentment. Her gentleness was legend, and I will always be grateful to have been born to such a spiritually gifted woman.

Sometime after Mother's transition, when I made the decision to move into her bedroom with the intention of imbibing her goodness, I discovered she had placed a small angel in front of a photograph of me with Sadie, a Lassie look-alike Collie I had given my parents for Christmas one year. Mother loved this dog almost as much as she loved Dad, or "RSJ," and me. When I spotted the angel, I was very glad I had selected a casket with an angel fastened to the satin to protect Mother in her journey with Jesus—as if these two needed any assistance from a still mortal being.

Jesus, a Jagadguru of enormous beauty and power, received my mother unto himself just as he said he would in John 14:3. Will I recognize her when she is returned to earth as the saint Jesus said she would be? Quite frankly, I don't know. She may be sent to a different part of the world to live out what I suspect may be her final incarnation as one who is sent back to earth, perhaps as a high level teacher. It is very difficult for me to believe I would not recognize Mother's gentle strength anywhere on earth, or in the world to come, should I have the good fortune to encounter her once more.

In saying he intended to return to earth, Jesus could have been urging his followers to stay awake and watch for him in the subtle realms such as those where I met him at the time of my mother's transition. Or, if Jesus took what Indian religions call *mahasamadhi,* the spiritual "merger" alluded to by Bishop Synesius in a previous paragraph, his energy could have poured back into the universe. As part of the pool of Siddhas, or saints, Jesus would still be able to communicate with his disciples, and his energy could be even stronger than it was on earth. If Jesus took *mahasamadhi,* he could return to the earth plane ethereally any time he wished to meet with his disciples as well as escort the faithful into Heaven as he did my Mother.

Mainstream Christians understandably might take issue with this view. "When?" some ask. "When, Lord?" some pray. "When, dear Jesus, are you going to return and make yourself visible to me?" some plead earnestly. If we take reincarnation seriously, there is no need to petition the Master for a glimpse of his form. If we take the resurrection as seriously as we do the crucifixion, we can learn to see the Lord with the eyes of the heart.

In light of what Oderberg calls "solid evidence" as to the existence of reincarnation in early Christianity, its rightful place in the contemporary Christian world merits further study. Quincy Howe, Jr. and Geddes MacGregor lend support to Oderberg's claims, and their texts exploring the validity of reincarnation in Christianity are worthy of reflection. The ability of the Christ to contact his disciples energetically while no longer living in a human body deserves further consideration as well, especially by Christians who invest in the spiritual practice of contemplation. In practical terms, and in language appealing to postmodern sensibility, Malcolm Boyd's *Are You Running with Me Jesus?* reflects the intimacy which can be experienced from contacting the Master by means of prayer.

Devotees of all major world religions might have difficulty recognizing their long transitioned Gurus should they reappear today. Since Jesus was Jewish by birth, he probably would look more like Jim Caviezel ("The Passion of the Christ," 2004) than the blue-eyed Jeffrey Hunter ("King of Kings," 1961) were he to come back in a human body similar to the one in which the historical Jesus lived. If Jesus appeared in the narthex of a Southern Baptist Church in Mississippi, who in the congregation would recognize the scruffy savior in tattered robes as their own?

Of course, this potential blind spot is not limited to Christianity. If the historical Buddha walked back into Sarnath tomorrow, he might go unnoticed among the Western tourists. Bhagawan Nityananda might be arrested if he appeared wearing only his loin cloth in some of the more clothes-conscious parts of the city. The passage of time matters as do cultural patterns and changes in fashion. The Lord in a torn robe or a swath of cotton might not qualify for the celebrity status afforded to some religious leaders in postmodern times.

By saying, "I am coming soon," Jesus might not have meant he would reappear in exactly the same form by which he was known in Biblical times. He might have meant he would reappear as "I am." The "I am" statements have attracted many interpretations, not least among them the notion of "I am" standing symbolically for someone much larger than the historical Jesus in human form. As a

Jagadguru of unquestionably purified consciousness, then surely Jesus surrendered his personal identity when he became enlightened. As a Siddha, or a Buddha, his claim, "I am the way, the truth, and the life" (John 14:6), likely emanated from a being who had dissolved all attachment to personality to live in a state of "luminous emptiness"—as Jagadgurus across religious traditions do.

Enlightenment is a process with well-documented levels, or tiers. Usually, enlightenment happens gradually as the Holy Spirit purifies the mind and heart. In saying, "I am the way, the truth, and the light," Jesus was letting the world know about his powers as a Shaktipat Guru, one who is capable of leading disciples across the stormy ocean of the world and up the tiers of purification into Paradise. He had the knowledge of how to awaken the Holy Spirit, and he wasn't shy about using it. Since the Holy Spirit is the Enlightener, any consciousness embodied in human form is capable of becoming a Christ, a Guru, a Buddha. Jesus was an example, not an exception. According to Colossians 3:4, "When Christ who is our life shall appear, then you also will be revealed with him in glory."

Christ, then, was not just a single man, an individual soul. He was, as Paramahansa Yogananda notes in *The Yoga of Jesus* (3, 7, 134), *Kutastha Chaitanya*, or the living breath of consciousness who was, and is, capable of lifting us all up to his level. In his ground breaking studies of the life and work of Jesus, Yogananda, as one of the first Indian Gurus to establish a *kula* or school in the West, is unusually sympathetic to the founder of Christianity. Believing that he encountered Jesus in the subtle realms, Yogananda recognizes Jesus as a Shaktipat Guru, but his language is slightly different. He writes mainly about the powerful vibrations which emanate from the mystic body of Jesus the

Christ.

Further, Christ is the state of consciousness which appears more often, perhaps, than many people of all faiths suspect to help human beings attain the very state embedded in the life of Jesus of Nazareth. When a consciousness becomes enlightened, it is the playing field, so to speak, of the saints. It bears the mark of "glory," defined here as "Christ consciousness," or a state of mind and being saturated with the peace which "passeth understanding" (Philippians 4:7).

The mission, *dharma,* or sacred purpose of such a purified consciousness is to help human beings free themselves from the traps of ego and snares of the world. Depending on the religious tradition, these beings are called apostles (Christianity), *adhi kari purushas* (Hinduism, the Hindu Tantra, and Yoga), and *bodhisattvas* (Buddhism). Sometimes they identify as Gurus in the public domain; sometimes they keep a lower profile. They do the work asked of them by their Master Teachers and lineages; they live as monastics, householders, and *brahmacharyas*, a third category of particular interest in the West where Indian religions have taken root.

Whether Christian, Hindu, or Buddhist, most sexually active disciples in the West are householders, that is, they live together in families or alternative family structures. As a Shambhala Buddhist Acharya and long time disciple of Chogyam Trungpa Rinpoche has said, householder *sadhana*, or spiritual practice, is the place "where the rubber meets the road." Similarly, life inside monasteries can present challenges. In one of her many interesting talks as a major figure and Acharya in Shambhala Buddhism, Ani Pema Chodron addresses the tensions which can arise inside Gampo Abbey, a Buddhist monastery located in Cape Breton, Nova Scotia, Canada. Friction among human beings living in community seems to be inevitable, even among monks, nuns, and *brahmacharyas* who have taken vows of celibacy. This very friction enhances the undoing of habitual patterns which can lead to what Christians call *synne*, a term from the Latin meaning to miss one's mark, or to the dissolution of karmic imprints.

Whether Jesus was married, celibate, or gay—and arguments exist to support all three claims about his sexual orientation—his life resembles that of Siddhartha Gautama who became the Buddha after he came to terms with suffering. Jesus was born a Jew in an area some now think of as the Fertile Crescent, and according to many Christians, his crucifixion represents the pinnacle in human suffering. Siddhartha was born a Hindu in north India, and although he was never nailed to a wooden cross, he suffered mightily from what the Shambhala Buddhists call "broken heartedness" in the face of human conflict. Surely Siddhartha must have experienced deep reservations when he left his wife and child to live the life of a wandering mendicant. But, he, like Jesus, was motivated by a compassion which called him to risk everything for humanity, not just his inner circle.

Whereas Jesus sought to revise the Judaism of his day, Siddhartha critiqued the older Indian religion for its focus on ritual to the exclusion of inner experience. The "outer" purity related to following the laws of Leviticus was no longer sufficient, according to Jesus in the chapter of Matthew. Likewise, Siddhartha insisted on taking the inward turn, working to eradicate internal delusions and lies, and teaching his disciples the value of mindfulness. Placing flower petals on statues while pretending to obey Brahmin priests was insufficient to the Buddha's new way of being.

Performing rituals might work to dissolve certain karmas and strengthen the subtle body, but ultimately, according to Buddhist thought—and neo-Hindu practice as well—we have to take the inward turn and face ourselves.

Siddhartha brought to the practice of mindfulness a wealth of spiritual knowledge from the older Indian tradition. Practicing Buddhists in the United States and Western Europe sometimes decline to acknowledge the impact of Siddhartha's training with two Hindu Gurus before he set off with five mendicants to live for a time as an ascetic. Arada Kalama and Udraka Ramaputra apparently saw great potential in Siddhartha since both reportedly asked him to serve as their successors. Siddhartha said no to these invitations, but as legend has it, he wanted Arada Kalama to know he had found the "Middle Way," or the path beyond suffering. It is probably no accident that Siddhartha transformed into the Buddha gave his first sermon on *Gurupurnima,* the fullest moon of the year celebrating the Guru. Arada Kalama allegedly died seven days after Siddhartha attained enlightenment, so his protégé could not return to the hermit-sage to share his newly found freedom and seek his teacher's confirmation.

It takes a Jagadguru to instigate the movement toward enlightenment. Therefore, Arada Kalama and Udraka Ramaputra may have been Shaktipat Gurus who had more to do with the creation of a Buddha, or another Shaktipat Guru, than they have been given credit for in the study of Asian religions. Siddhartha allegedly felt dissatisfied when he left the ashrams of Arada Kalama and Udraka Ramaputra, but restlessness is a stage on the path to enlightenment and usually signifies a need for more spiritual work. Siddhartha's continuing search at this stage of his *sadhana* or spiritual practice does not necessarily speak to the

the inadequacy of his Hindu teachers.

Usually, Siddhartha's dissatisfaction is attributed to the Gurus with whom he studied when such may not have been the case. Blaming Gurus is a common practice and is not restricted to the Buddha's time. Guru Arada may have planted the seed which then was given a watering, or a boost, by Guru Udraka. The seed then blossomed that fateful night when Siddhartha experienced the formless, or thought-free state, which Arada Kalama was noted for teaching. Prior to his experience in Bodh Gaya, Siddhartha simply could not "get there," so to speak, because his thoughts were still overly active.

Arada Kalama and Udraka Ramaputra would not have called themselves Shaktipat Gurus. In the sixth century before the common era, Shaktipat had not yet emerged as a primary term for the awakening of the holy energy. By the ninth century common era, when Abhinavagupta did his ground-breaking work in Kashmir, not far from the birthplace of the Buddha, the term used for the great energy was *visarga-shakti.* It is as yet unclear as to when the term Shakatipat came "above ground" from the oral tradition into print, but according to Professor Paul Muller Ortega, the sacred energy is included in the 13th Ahnika of Abhinavagupta's germinal text, the *Tantraloka.*

As with many ancient figures, much in the life of Siddhartha the Buddha remains unresolved. Commentators sometimes reproduce information which could be examined more critically. According to Alexander Berzin, for instance, we are not certain if Siddhartha, a member of the warrior caste, was born into a royal family. His princely situation, Berzin notes, seems to have been a rather late addition to the biographical accounts constructed by his monks.

Uncertainty as to the spiritual education of Jesus exists in Christianity as well. Some say he was trained as a rabbi; others think he was raised as a Jew and then lived on the edges of Jewish law, perhaps in an Essene community. Like the Buddha, Jesus is sometimes treated as if he arrived on earth already equipped as a Jagadguru, but the suffering in his life suggests otherwise. No less than Siddhartha Gautama the Buddha, Jesus was tempted in the desert by the devil who is a direct equivalent of Mara, the Buddha's temptress. Like Siddhartha, Jesus fought off the assault, or in Christian terms, warded off the temptation.

The 40 days and nights Jesus spent in the Judaean Desert are written about in the chapters of Matthew, Mark, and Luke. Different interpretations of the 40 days exist, and one of the most compelling for contemporary times, perhaps, is John Howard Yoder's. Jesus, according to Yoder, may have been confronted in the desert by a temptation to power, particularly political power. Given that Jesus was drawn to the poor and disenfranchised, this claim has merit. Indeed, Jesus was up against a corrupt Roman hierarchy, and he was at heart a revolutionary.

At the same time, Jesus's 40 days in the desert can be read as a time of solitary retreat. Having been baptized by John, he might have needed reprieve from the intense heat of the Holy Spirit. Jesus, in the desert, could have been thrust into an intense period of self-examination. If understood in Yoder's terms, the desire for power could have been a driving force Jesus was called upon to release or transmute.

Who was Jesus's Arada Kalama? Was he John the Baptist, perhaps, or an unseen Kabbalist hiding in the desert near the Dead Sea, or behind the thick robes of an ordained rabbi known as a *smicha* or *semicha* (pronounced smee-ha)? Were a Jagadguru involved in Jesus's training as a Shaktipat

Guru, would he necessarily have been visible?

Siddhartha might not have been in the presence of Arada Kalama or Udraka Ramaputra when the seed of Shaktipat fell. If they were legitimate Gurus, they could have given Shaktipat and guided the sacred power at will—by *sankalpa* from a distance. Siddhartha might not have recognized the whisperings of Mara who assaulted him as the voices of two Gurus disguised. The voices were not necessarily those of Arada Kalama or Udraka Ramaputra, but Gurus have been known to take other forms for purposes of testing their disciples, sometimes to the point of distraction. An intense assault often takes place for certain sensibilities during the so-called "time of fruition" to be explored later in this text.

Siddhartha was in no mood to give full credit to the older Indian tradition, but in the final analysis, Arada Kalama and Udraka Ramaputra may have had more to do with his enlightenment than contemporary Buddhist practitioners and scholars have been willing to grant. If he received Shaktipat from either or both of these Gurus, they would have been honor-bound by tradition to guide him to liberation.

Similarly, if Jesus were trained by a *smicha*, he probably became a *smicha* himself. Jesus is thought by some theorists to have studied for some fifteen to eighteen years in a rabbinical school with a rabbi with *smicha,* or authority. These rabbinical teachers were allowed to interpret the scriptures and teach disciples, and their perspectives were considered to be insightful. According to the second chapter of Luke, Jesus at age twelve was discovered by his parents with the elders in the Temple shortly before he went missing for a period of some 15 to 18 years. The Bible does not tell us if the elders, possibly *smicha*, gave Jesus instructions as to where to go next for his studies.

Jesus could have been called from afar by the wise men who attended his birth in Bethlehem. After all, they came on camels bearing spices from another country. The wise men could, indeed, have had their origins in India or Tibet, and the Indo-Tibetan theory of Jesus's whereabouts will be addressed in greater detail in a later chapter. For now, suffice it to cite India as the country best known for the gift of Shaktipat, and Jesus could have traveled there on the trade routes.

At the end of his life, as he hung on the cross, Jesus understandably said he felt "forsaken." For an instant, as recorded in Matthew 27:45-46, he seems to have experienced separation from the Father, and perhaps from the *smicha,* whether Jewish, Indian, or Tibetan, who had been instrumental in his training. The *smicha* may have given Jesus one final test before the crucified Master "ascended into heaven," or experienced full blown enlightenment, which comes only at the time of *mahasamadhi,* according to some commentators.

In any case, could there be any test more laden with anguish than doubt just prior to expiration? That is, if Jesus felt anxiety as he was dying. By virtue of his elevated consciousness, one theory holds, Jesus may have been able to transcend the pain of being nailed to the cross. If such a theory holds any validity, no further evidence would be needed to establish Jesus as the highest kind of Jagadguru.

The energy of the Jagadguru leads disciples to *moksha,* or freedom. Both Jesus and Siddhartha became Shaktipat Gurus, and it is very difficult, if not impossible, to attain the Master's state without a Shaktipat Guru at the helm.

CHAPTER II

Gifts of the Holy Spirit: Foremost Omniscience

As Thich Nhat Hanh notes in *You Are Here*, the Buddha's energy is the equivalent of the Holy Spirit. In other words, Buddha energy is Shakti, to use the Indian term, and Shakti is no different from the Guru or Jesus. Further, according to the Vietnamese Buddhist monk who has attracted a large following in the West, the virtues associated with the Holy Spirit—understanding, healing, and compassion—are also accompanied by varying degrees of omniscience.

"Let this mind be in you, which was also in Christ Jesus," asserts Philippians 2:5. Said another way, let Buddha mind or Christ consciousness be in you. This command is very close to the Yogic instruction to "imbibe the Guru," or to take into yourself the Guru principle as a state of unwavering steadiness.

"This mind" of Jesus the Christ was made of omniscience and humility. In its beautiful simplicity, it was like the mind described in *Zen Mind, Beginner's Mind*, the title of a now famous text by Shunryu Suzuki Roshi, the Soto Zen Buddhist monk who brought his teachings to the United States in the 1950s. Like the Roshis, Lamas, and Jagadgurus, Jesus the Christ was capable of continual astonishment. So others can be, too, when awareness is focused on "whatsoever things are honest . . . whatsoever things are lovely . . . whatsoever things are of good report" (Philippians 4:8). The cleaner the mind, the more clearly it can reflect the gifts of the Holy Spirit.

Although some Christians regard Jesus as the only way to salvation, or freedom, Interfaith scholars believe that Master Teachers on par with Jesus have lived, and continue to live, in parts of the world outside the "Holy Land." India and Tibet are no less "holy" than Israel to disciples of Bhagawan Nityananda and His Holiness the Dalai Lama. "This mind which was in Jesus" is not restricted by geographical boundaries and does not seem to prefer deserts over mountains and coastal areas.

Hinduism, the major religion of India, includes Jesus as an avatar, or a major spiritual teacher. Interestingly, Christianity generally does not include the Indian Gurus or Buddhist Lamas and Roshis in its stable of great teachers. Certain forms of fundamentalist Christianity are more provincial than the Asian religions as they appear after importation into the United States. In an age when Interfaith and Interspiritual mappings are on the cutting edge of theological studies, it helps to see all religions as existing on an equal plane. If "this mind which was in Jesus" can also be in you, and presumably in me, then surely "this mind" can also be in the non-Christian Master Teachers whose job it is to guide their students to liberation.

The tendency to elevate Jesus over other Master Teachers is understandable, perhaps, since Jesus was such a powerful being. Jesus was omniscient, he performed miracles, and his ability to attract disciples has lasted over two millennia. When a religion has such a potent Master Teacher or Shaktipat Guru at its core, it is, indeed, fortunate, but if it engages in exclusive truth claims, they can harden into dogma.

Such is the danger inherent in some forms of Christianity. Christianity's attitude of superiority, especially in the United States, is compounded when its scripture, the *Holy Bible*, is held up as containing the only truth. How could this be so when the Hindu scriptures date back thousands of years? The *Rig Veda*, for instance, dates to somewhere between 500 and 1,500 BCE. Are theologians and spiritual practitioners supposed to dispose of the older scriptures when new ones arrive or are discovered as the Dead Sea Scrolls were long after the Christian canon had been established? Such disregard for religious history diminishes rather than enhances the study of religion, and ironically, reduces Christianity's Master Teacher to less than he might be on a world stage alongside other beings of equal stature.

Certain sects of neo-Hinduism and Buddhism can exhibit attitudes of superiority as well, especially in regions outside their homelands. Christian born Buddhists who leave the church for a set of teachings with presumably greater intellectual substance are, perhaps, more prone to this tendency than others. Buddhism is probably not at fault for its practitioners being somewhat arrogant with regard to the spiritual immaturity of Christian narratives. The tendency to judge intellectually cuts across the world's religions, but may be more pronounced among Buddha's followers, because Buddhism is closer to being a philosophy/psychology governed by reason than it is to being a theistic religion.

Interfaith/Interspiritual/Intra-Tantric Studies can be useful in helping to diminish the sense of spiritual superiority which often accompanies entrenchment in dogma. By promoting the virtues of intra-religious dialogue, the Interfaith Movement has assisted many people in the process of learning how to think across religious boundaries, thus avoid the traps of fundamentalism. When individuals step outside their story lines, or personal narratives partially constructed by religious upbringing, they usually are able to develop more expansive perspectives.

At the same time, the Interfaith Movement itself

must be careful not to succumb to the allure of intellectual and political superiority. Commitment to a movement can assume even more importance than involvement in a religious system. If "insider" teachers and events amass more clout than spiritual teachings and practices, then it might be time to re-evaluate the situation.

The human ego has a mischievous way of making its list of priorities appear to be sacred when they can be alternate forms of selfishness and self-absorption in disguise. All the religious traditions as well as their critics and correctives need to be wary of self-congratulations. As a neo-Hindu Guru once said, what we want can easily become what we believe to be right.

Religions other than Christianity have their miracle makers, too. For example, Bhagawan Nityananda, a modern day saint from south India, is said to have performed miracles similar to those of Jesus the Christ. A parallel exists between the loaves and fishes Jesus multiplied to feed the masses, as reported in all four gospels, and the money Nityananda produced, as if by magic, to pay workers who were building a temple in Kanhangad, not far from Mangalore, India. To the alarm of local officials, Nityananda reportedly dove to the bottom of a pond and then surfaced, laughing, his fists filled with rupees. Like Jesus, Nityananda was said to have walked on water. Jesus may have shared "this mind" with Nityananda even though the Indian Jagadguru lived nearly twenty centuries after his Christian predecessor.

Jesus, like Bhagawan Nityananda and Master Teachers in other religions, knew without seeing with his physical eyes. When preparing to go to his death on what is now known as Palm Sunday, Jesus turned to two disciples and said, in effect, "Go, get me that donkey" (Matthew

21:1-2). Jesus could see no donkey standing down the road, but he knew the animal waited in a nearby village.

Did Jesus have the donkey reserved with its owner before dispatching his men to bring the colt to him? Christian ministers continue to be fascinated by the role of the donkey in Jesus's triumphal ride into the city. One has dared to ask, "How did Jesus know the donkey would be there?"

In an online essay, John Stanko, minister, blogger, and life coach, asks whether or not Jesus's knowledge of the donkey's location could have represented a "gift of the Spirit," the Holy Spirit which disseminates knowledge through super-natural or mystical means.

In addition to sight, the Holy Spirit's other gifts are listed in the book of Isaiah. They include wisdom, understanding, right judgment, courage, spiritual knowledge, reverence, and awe. They are similar to the gifts mentioned by Buddhist teacher Thich Nhat Hanh earlier in this chapter.

Some twelve centuries after the death of Jesus, St. Thomas Aquinas explored the "gifts of the Spirit" in greater detail in his now classic text, the *Summa Theologica.* St. Thomas Aquinas is the Dante of Roman Catholic theology, and his work has influenced many religious thinkers, including the Southern American fiction writer Flannery O'Connor, who claimed to have kept a copy of the *Summa* on her bedside table.

If we read Jesus as a Jagadguru, the answer to John Stanko's question is clearly yes. Not only did Jesus know where the donkey waited, but he also knew the owner would not object to loaning the animal out to his Lord. Jesus probably reserved the donkey by transmission. The donkey itself behaved better than most donkeys do when they have yet to be ridden (Luke 19:37, John 12:17-18). His cooperative demeanor is not surprising since animals tend to be calm in the presence of Jagadgurus. An Indian Jagadguru, for example, famously tamed a wild elephant. Another Indian Jagadguru was photographed next to a large deer who sat still as stone for the camera.

Once, when an Indian Jagadguru was in Mexico City, she, having no map or former knowledge of streets in one of the world's largest metropolises, gave directions to a taxi driver. As the story goes, travelers in the car were amazed when their automobile pulled up in front of the correct address. It was as if this Jagadguru had a built-in GPS.

Similarly, and more importantly, certain Indian Jagadgurus are said to have the power to read not only their disciples' thoughts, but also the *samskaras*, or karmic imprints, in their subtle bodies. In this respect, some Indian Jagadgurus and the Buddhist Rinpoches share certain powers not unlike those of Jesus who knew which disciple would betray him for a few pieces of silver. Buddhists chant for the omniscience experienced by Master Teachers to be granted to all.

Of course, we all have this power to some extent, and we all, most likely, have at one time or another suspected a friend or relative of reading our thoughts. The late Elva Jones, for one, had an uncanny ability to finish my sentences. Often, as we were sitting at the breakfast table, planning the day's activities, Mother demonstrated her omniscience. It was as if she could reach in and tell me what I was thinking. As reflected in the biblical story of Jesus and the donkey, Jagadgurus have developed this ability to the nth degree.

"And Jesus knew their thoughts"—it is written in

Matthew 12:25 at the start of a verse which speaks to the ways in which a "city or house divided against itself shall not stand." The second part of this verse is quoted frequently. The metaphor of a "divided house" is clear, especially as a sign of dualistic thinking, but what about the way in which the divided house is introduced? Who sees into the house? None other than Jesus, omniscient Jagadguru who is capable of reading the interior lives of his disciples.

Devotees who turn away in fear of the Master's powers, or in anger and disgust, rarely stop to ask if the Guru knows their motives. Just as Jesus knew Judas would betray him, and Peter would deny him, so modern day Masters are said to have knowledge of the future. They know which disciples will stay and which will go, which will be true and which will sell their spiritual inheritance for a romantic adventure or a literary reputation.

"And Jesus knew their thoughts" . . . how many times have Christians heard this line from Matthew 12:25 discussed in terms of Jesus having omniscient powers? Many Christians speak in terms of walking and talking with Jesus, but the thought of the Lord being a mind reader for Christians unfamiliar with the pagan tradition may place him in the company of so-called "witches" and "sorcerers." Since the Master is supposedly available when called from anywhere on earth, his omniscient faculties may not be all that different from the power of witches who were hanged in 17th century New England. Such power often strikes at the heart of fear in the masculine logos.

If Jesus were omniscient, then he was capable of fixing a "divided house" without much help from the carpenters, a certain theological position holds. Such a stance may stop short of involving human beings in the work of their own salvation. It may fail to foreground the Holy Spirit's role in the process of purification.

Salvation, for a good many Christians, is thought to be prompted by Grace. Grace alone, they say, can repair the "divided house." This view is backed by scriptures such as Ephesians 2:8: "For by Grace you have been saved through faith, and that not of yourself; it is the gift of God, not of works, lest anyone should boast." When understood for less than it says, such a theology can exempt human beings from having to take responsibility for their own spiritual growth. Unfortunately, Christians who "boast" of being saved by grace sometimes tend to discount the faith of others in non-Christian traditions.

A woman who came to Slate Branch Ashram to take a class did not stay very long for fear she might have to put forth more self-effort than she was prepared to exert. She arrived late, with no text for the course, complaining about too little time for lunch and too much traffic.

"Why should I sit around with my eyes shut?" she asked. "All I have to do is believe in Jesus. I don't have to do anything. Jesus has already done all the work for me."

Now, this woman's pastor might take kindly to her attitude, but we have to wonder. She was cantankerous throughout the course, she interrupted other participants, and she presented her ideas as not-to-be-questioned truth. She sincerely believed she was saved by Grace, and no further work on her part was needed.

On the other hand, some Christians work on themselves constantly. They amplify Sunday school and church services with scriptural study. When their churches are not in session, they attend other churches. Some go to synagogues and mosques as well. They belong to Interfaith dialogue groups designed to open intra-religious conversation. If they encounter internal difficulties, they seek the help of a spiritual counselor or a good therapist.

Another woman comes to Slate Branch regularly with a highly positive attitude. Although she drives several hours from her home in the northeastern United States, she arrives with a cheerful smile on her face, ready to offer seva. A Roman Catholic convert, this woman seems to understand the Interfaith perspective without really trying. She helps others, too. Others seem to gravitate to her good heartedness as she sits in the dining room, quietly sipping tea. She even gifted the ashram with a sparkling white teapot!

Some Christians may be baffled by the comparison of salvation to enlightenment. Certainly, the levels of salvation are foreign to many contemporary Protestants. Tiers of salvation as well as damnation exist in *The Divine Comedy*, published in the year 1300, a year of Jubilee in the Roman Catholic Church when the concept of Purgatory still had considerable currency.

My own spiritual journey attests to a strong correspondence between salvation and enlightenment. Unquestionably, my journey has been marked by certain levels and tiers along the way.

I was christened into a United Methodist Church in south central Kentucky at the age of accountability. Although I went through instruction, I did not fully understand the meaning of the Christian message. I can remember standing at the Easter altar in my broad-brimmed, flying saucer hat I suspected the boys might try to use as a frisbee after church. "I don't know what this is about," I recall thinking.

Later, I attended a revival at First Baptist Church in my hometown. The preacher's words and the hymns were so convincing that I rose from my seat and walked down the aisle. I was baptized into the faith of my Grandfathers and went to church there through my high school years.

In college, as I became a budding intellectual, I began to fall away from Christianity. Interested in philosophy, I thrilled to the rhapsodic prose of Henri Bergson. I took a course in comparative world religions, and when my professor said, "Hinduism is the only religion in the world that can take anything into itself," I felt a spark—a sense of recognition. This was my first exposure to the Indian tradition in which I would eventually become ordained as a monk in the Saraswati order.

After my first crack at graduate school in the early 1970s, I moved to Atlanta. I wanted to be in the world where the action was happening. Deeply political, I came awake during the women's movement, and no patriarch was about to tell me who to worship or how. As Rev. Deefholts notes in her "Introduction" to *Jesus Was a Shaktipat Guru*, I was part of a generation that had put interest in conventional religion on hold—in suspension. My spiritual sustenance came from reading and writing poetry, and I was introduced to Hatha Yoga during my senior year in college.

In August of 1978, I experienced a cataclysmic spiritual conversion, which ultimately showed me to the rungs of the spiritual ladder. It was an intense time. I was experiencing anxiety so acute one muggy night—all I could think to do was pray.

"Please remove this anguish," I pleaded quietly.

I had no idea to what or to whom I was praying.

"Please remove this anguish," I said over and over again.

As I spoke these words repeatedly, I could feel the anguish being lifted out of my body. It felt as if something or someone had gotten hold of the tensions and pushed them out of my belly up through the top of my head. Simultaneously, like Paul on the road to Damascus, I experienced an inflooding of light. The next morning, I felt brand new.

I had no idea what had happened to me, so I went back to Emory University in search of some explanations. I wound up doing an interdisciplinary doctorate and making a decision to seek a teaching position in a liberal arts setting. Not until August of 1988, some 10 years after the conversion experience, did I encounter the great redeeming mantra, *Om Namah Shivaya.*

On that sweltering late summer night in Georgia, I had experienced a Kundalini awakening, but I did not know at the time what it was. The Holy Spirit had roused from her slumber. Windhorse had gently flown out over the mountains, and I was on my way to getting free of the automatic patterns which had coagulated in my mind, heart, and body, to create such anxiety.

The anguish never returned, I am happy to say. But, I had more work to do to dissolve certain obstacles standing in the way of freedom. I could have looked at August 1978 as a moment of Grace—no more effort needed—but had I done so, I would have realized only a fraction of omniscience available to all who undergo purification willingly.

Invariably, the Holy Spirit will lead us to salvation, or enlightenment, but she is more effective when she has the cooperation of subjects who are willing to do the hard work of freedom. Without willingness, the sacred energy can go no further than *Ajna* chakra, the so-called "third eye," or vertical axis of the cross. To attain freedom and wear a crown of thorns, we must be totally crucified, ego subsumed and stripped of its ability to mask "this mind" which is also "in Christ Jesus."

From *Ajna* chakra, the so-called "command center," omniscience is enhanced as Maha Kundalini Shakti, or the Holy Spirit, makes her way to the *Sahasrara.* In the chakras above *Ajna,* the powers of omniscience increase. When stabilized in the crown chakra, the work is complete. The kingdom of heaven is at hand.

Ajna is also the center through which commands and instructions from the Guru are received. Sometimes, they take the form of actual words, and sometimes, they appear as images. Whether we hear words may depend on how verbal we tend to be. If our strengths are visual, then we probably will receive through *Ajna* in images and symbols, possibly dreams. Some people receive in both ways.

My first experience with material coming in through *Ajna* chakra happened after I attended my first Shaktipat Intensive at an ashram in northern California in June of 1989. I had a number of questions, and after the Intensive, an image of the Guru appeared on my mental screen and patiently answered my questions, all of them, one by one. The Guru who conducted the Shaktipat Intensive was still in California, and I was in Pennsylvania.

One of my most remarkable experiences at *Ajna* chakra during my years of *sadhana* happened at an ashram in upstate New York during the high holiday known as Maha Shivaratri. After this experience, there was no doubt in my mind as to the Guru's omniscience as well as my ability to receive commands.

It was beginning to snow, and I was feeling a strong desire to get on the road back down Highway 17 to northwestern Pennsylvania. As I was packing my clothes, I heard, "Come to the central hall before you leave."

The words were so clear that I looked around to see if the Guru was in the room with me.

"I can't come to the central hall," I thought. "It's snowing, and I really must get on the road now."

I heard the words again.

"Come to the central hall before you leave."

It was six hours, minimum, back to Meadville, Pennsylvania. In the snow, it would take longer. It surely would be safer to start driving than go to another building and try to make my way through the crowd usually surrounding the Guru. The snow drifts across upstate New York would surely mount as I skidded toward Lake Erie.

I heard the words one last time.

"Come to the central hall before you leave."

Clothes finally packed, I made my way out through the courtyard to the side of the café and flower shop and in the back door of a building considered to be central to the ashram complex.

There sat the Guru. She was sitting in the small room where she normally received disciples and guests. Nobody was near. In those days, seeing the Guru all by herself was highly unusual.

I went as close to the Guru as I felt comfortable going. She turned to face me. She looked worried—as if she intended to drive with me in the snow. We sat together in silence for several minutes. No words were spoken. It felt to me as if we merged into the mystic heart as one being.

When people became aware of the Guru's presence, they began to gather around. The Guru looked away from me and began speaking with others. Slowly, I pranamed, or bowed, and made my way back out into the snow. The trudge to my car in UGG boots was made much lighter by the command at *Ajna* I almost did not answer—as was the long drive home.

According to Tantric teachings, when the sacred energy reaches *Ajna* chakra, there is no turning back to the ego-driven life, or the life in which *ahamkara* struggles for control. Perhaps this was the Guru's message as we sat together in silence that February morning.

At *Ajna,* the Jagadguru takes over the reins, and habitual patterns which remain to block the light from shining through will be dissolved in time. In the Yogic traditions, disciples say the Guru must ask the disciple's permission to penetrate *Rudra Granthi*, the knot at *Ajna*, and go on up through the string of chakras leading to the *Sahasrara.* When the question was posed to me, I said yes immediately.

Jagadgurus can guide the Kundalini Shakti, or Holy Spirit, from any distance just as the Guru did with me and others after our first Shaktipat Intensives. Gurus do not have to be physically present in the lives of disciples to do this sacred work. For Christians, omniscience is especially significant since Jesus is no longer living in human form. As Jesus did with his first apostles, Jagadgurus also work through disciples who act as conduits for the sacred power. Disciples who are tapped to disperse the Shakti must undergo extensive training. This training can take place in the presence of the Guru or through a network in consciousness which includes other disciples who have attained omniscient faculties. In Christian terminology, this kind of mystical communication is known as the "communion of saints." Among ordained clergy, it is known as Apostolic Succession.

As demonstrated by his knowledge of where the

donkey waited and which disciple would betray him, it is clear: Jesus had the gift of sight. Omniscience is a tell-tale characteristic of Shaktipat Gurus, and no Guru worth his or her lineage would use the power of omniscience haphazardly.

CHAPTER III

Guru as 'Troublemaker'

According to Ani Pema Chodron, the "national treasure" of Shambhala Buddhism, as she has been called by Sakyong Mipham Rinpoche, Gurus can be "troublemakers." More often than not, they give us what they know we need rather than what we think we would like to have. They put us in a position to examine the automatic patterns we hold most dear.

Ani Pema delights in recalling how Chogyam Trungpa employed Guru tactics common to virtually all Master Teachers. Once, when she approached Rinpoche, longing for his approval, he looked away with a bored expression on his face. No one can see inside a Guru's intentions, but Trungpa Rinpoche may well have presented his student who was longing for his attention with the gift of a cold shoulder to begin preparing her as a world class teacher. Who knows for certain?

Jesus manifested troublemaker tendencies in several different ways. Certainly, he was at his troublemaker best when he got down off the donkey's back and confronted the money changers in his Father's house. Recorded in all four gospels of the New Testament, the "Cleansing of the Temple" takes place at the time of Passover when thousands of people were present in the city. While Jesus's rebuke was directed at the money changers specifically, it surely must have been a lesson for all who witnessed the Master's fierce injunction to stop the commercial exchange in this holiest of places.

Where confronting greed is concerned, Jesus was no less a troublemaker than Chogyam Trungpa Rinpoche who asked his disciples to examine the spiritual materialism embedded in culture and cocoon, a Shambhala Buddhist term for the "wrap" we live in made of social and familial patterns. In fact, Jesus's attitude toward money is another argument in support of possible Essene connections. Commentators are fairly certain the Essenes used no money in their cultural exchange.

Jesus was a troublemaker in five distinctly troublemaking ways:

1) He wrote nothing.
2) He called for a new order.
3) He challenged both rules and rituals.
4) He was a political revolutionary.
5) He was a Shaktipat Guru.

When we examine these five claims, we find they all could play a part in Jesus's motives. While the "Cleansing of the Temple" may have been the culminating event which led to the Master's crucifixion, other troublemaking factors were at work as well.

Jesus wrote nothing, and nothing was written about him for quite some time after his death. What better way to make trouble for future historians than to leave no record?

Of course, many Christians consider the New Testament to be absolute truth with regard to the life and teachings of Jesus. Even a cursory look at passages related to Jesus's troublemaking proclivities reveals the risk we take in reading the New Testament literally. Certain sections, including the "Cleansing of the Temple," depict a man who was quick to anger. More than likely, Jesus as a Jagadguru, displayed some fire which others interpreted as anger. A true Jagadguru would find anger as much a waste of emotional energy as fear.

Jesus's leaving no written records has an upside, too.

In addition to providing a wealth of life lessons, the New Testament, which was written by others after Jesus's death, can be read and discussed, time and again, for its literary richness. It will continue to provide work for Religious Studies scholars for years to come. Now that Christianity has interfaced with the other major religions, new insights can be brought to bear on Jesus's motives, his possible political affiliations, and the words he allegedly spoke.

Jesus asked human beings to be better than they were. He asked the people of his day to seek the kingdom within rather than invest their hopes for happiness in sensual pleasures and political power.

According to Jesus's recorded words, we must live by higher standards than those set by the world. "Be perfect, therefore as your heavenly father is perfect," Jesus reportedly said in Matthew 5:48. Further, the kind of perfection which Jesus advised is "impossible" with humankind, but "with God all things are possible." (Matthew 19:26).

In other words, the impossible becomes possible for those who receive the power of the Holy Spirit from Jesus the Christ. The Holy Spirit assists Jesus in his troublemaking activities. It is the Holy Spirit who actually does the work of purification leading to perfection. The Holy Spirit is a troublemaker par excellence.

Jesus challenged the exaggerated concern with ritual, restrictions and the fine points of Law. He sought to turn the tide away from the proliferation of rules.

"Woe to you, Scribes and Pharisees, Hypocrits!" are the words Jesus supposedly spoke when he confronted the Pharisees in Matthew 23. He accused the Pharisees of refining their taste buds by "tithing mint and dill and cumin" while neglecting "justice and mercy and faith."

Moreover, Jesus accused the Pharisees of being more interested in dancing on the head of a legalistic pin than in showing compassion and taking action to address the nation's extreme poverty.

In one of the most provocative metaphors of the New Testament, the author of Matthew 23 has Jesus compare the Pharisees to "whitewashed tombs, which outwardly appear beautiful, but within they are full of dead men's bones and all uncleanliness."

Jesus, troublemaking Jagadguru, could see inside the hearts and minds of those who invested too much in rules and too little in love for friends and foes alike.

Jesus was a political agitator capable of inciting the Zealots. At least the Romans who ruled Palestine seemed to think so. According to some scholarly accounts, Jesus may have been a Zealot himself.

The question as to whether or not Jesus was a Zealot is thorny, particularly since Zealotry may not have crystallized as a movement until the first century after his death. Nonetheless, several of Jesus's disciples were known Zealots who took issue with Roman philosophy, some commentators suggest.

The disciple who betrayed Jesus for a few pieces of silver, according to James Still, was a Zealot. His name, Judas Iscariot, is a corruption of the Latin "sicarius," or "knife-man," a common Roman reference to Zealots. Jesus equipped his followers with swords in anticipation of trouble (Luke 22:36-38), Still notes. At least one of Jesus's supporters scuffled with Temple police to help in resisting Jesus's arrest (Mark 14:47), Still adds.

In setting forth his argument for Jesus as a Zealot, Still says Gospel accounts may be trying to smooth over Jesus's political mission. Indeed, such is a fascinating theory, for Jesus appears to have been keenly aware of the political factions of his time.

In light of Still's claim with regard to possible white washing, it is interesting to take note of Reza Aslan's 2013 book entitled *Zealot: The Life and Times of Jesus of Nazareth. Zealot* zoomed to the top of the bestseller list after Aslan was interviewed on Fox TV.

Jesus lived among the poorest of the poor, Aslan claims, and became a pedagogue of the oppressed. Aslan portrays Jesus as a knife-carrying Zealot, a position critiqued by Rev. Howard Bess who sees Jesus as being more dramatic than violent. According to Bess, Jesus was into "street theater;" his actions were designed to attract attention and make a point.

While Jesus and his disciples may have been involved in the formative stages of a movement which gained greater momentum in the first century of the common era, the Pharisees and Romans were invested in finding ways to diminish the Master's power. Jesus was a revolutionary, and revolutionaries are threatening to the status quo. But, his power exceeded the bounds of political motivation. Jesus was out not only to cleanse the Temple in Jerusalem, but also to create a revolution in the hearts and minds of all he encountered.

Most importantly, Jesus was a Shaktipat Guru. Shaktipat Gurus are rarely safe from convention and often stand in danger of being crucified—if not literally, then by public ridicule. Their intentions are of the highest, and not infrequently, people do not wish to be drug up to their level. It is comforting to remain mired in the mud. While the Pharisees and Romans were concerned with Jesus threatening their authority, his authority was based on the law of love.

A common characteristic of Shaktipat Gurus manifests in their love for children. In the 10th chapter of Mark, Jesus's disciples tried to move the children away from the Master, but Jesus said, "Let the children come unto me, do not hinder them, for to such belongs the Kingdom of God." Apparently wishing to reinforce his point, Jesus continued: "I say to you whoever does not receive the Kingdom of God like a child shall not enter it." Jesus took the children in his arms and blessed them, laying hands on them, giving them Shaktipat by touch.

Jesus resembles contemporary Jagadgurus in ways both obvious and subtle. For instance, the Indian Guru Amma not only takes children in her arms, but she also is known for getting grown men and women up in her lap and treating them like children. While some Westerners might be embarrassed, others enjoy the troublemaking play of the so-called "Hugging Guru." Amma's message is very like that of Jesus the Christ who instructed people to "Love your enemies and pray for those who persecute you" (Matthew 5: 44-45). It is difficult to imagine Amma ever meeting or creating an enemy although she, like other modern Gurus, has her detractors.

Where records of Jesus's troublemaking are concerned, disputations exist among scholars as to what material may have been intentionally removed from or unintentionally left out of the Christian scriptures. As the church sought to establish its foundation as an institution, well-meaning church fathers may have wished to portray Jesus as a peaceful Buddha to dilute his fierce rabbi tendencies. His troublemaking proclivities were obvious as he sought to overturn both the rigidity of Jewish law and Roman corruption.

As a Shaktipat Guru, Jesus was made of as much

fire as gentleness. Accordingly, the Master most likely ruffled a few feathers when he called his disciples to account for themselves. He not only kicked the money changers out of the Temple, but he also chided his disciples when he felt they needed instruction. As both Jews and Romans came into the presence of Jesus's undeniable heat, some must have sought to keep the sacred energy outside themselves. The collective resistance to Jesus and the Holy Spirit moving in his blood got him killed. Letting Jesus live would have meant a cleansing far more intense than the Holy Land was prepared to undergo at that time in history.

And Jesus knew their thoughts as do certain Indian Jagadgurus and Buddhist Rinpoches. The question is: how? Are Gurus born psychics? Some are born; some are made. Whether born omniscient, or polished in the fire, those who attain this level of spiritual development cannot get there without assistance from our old friend the Holy Ghost—the flying horse who knows how to gallop with the winds.

Carolyn Gimian, an early student of Chogyam Trungpa Rinpoche and editor of his collected works, notes in the March 2011 issue of *Shambhala Sun*, "Tapping into the energy of Windhorse is like generating your own solar power . . . through the practice of meditation we begin to realize that we have this inherent power or energy."

As the sacred energy penetrates *Ajna*, the energy vortex located just behind the brow, spiritual seekers grow in their abilities to read the vibrations of consciousness. Reading vibrations is also helpful to Gurus in their troublemaking activities.

Sometimes, disciples do not recognize what is going on when a Guru moves in as troublemaker. The tendencies are to blame and withdraw, or to withdraw and blame.

I once heard a story about a woman, a

contemporary money changer, who valued her material possessions greatly. She relished arriving at her roshi's zendo in a limo and then seeking out the most affluent disciples in residence. Intuitively, she was drawn into an office of the zendo to help with fundraising. Then, the woman was encouraged to establish a fundraising office in her hometown. Suddenly, she was informed that her services would no longer be needed. Sadly, she closed the office, and, in dismay, left her teacher's fold. To my knowledge, she never saw the connection between her own wish to be thought of as wealthy and the troublemaking situation she was given as a learning opportunity.

As one who used to rail against money and the acquisition of material goods, not uncommon in my Baby Boomer generation, I sympathize with the woman who loved limos. I had a reverse problem to face with regard to the material world.

One day at a retreat center outside New York City, a spiritual seeker said to me, you look like a million dollars. I was startled. I didn't look very good in those days. In the throes of purification, I had gained too much weight. My eyes were red, and I was beginning to show the effects of aging.

Not long after that incident, another seeker came walking toward me with greenbacks pinned all over her dress. I still laugh when I recall the way she looked in her paper money personification. The importance of managing money sensibly had to walk straight into my line of vision for me to get the message.

It's no wonder I wound up managing a retreat ashram in southern Kentucky where the deity in residence is Shri Maha Lakshmi, goddess of abundance and prosperity. Now that I have taken monastic vows in the Saraswati order, I can own nothing. But, it takes a fair amount of money to be able to put on programs for other people to enjoy. In my role as Spiritual Director, I must constantly discern where the fine lines are between being a monk and heading an ashram.

Shri Maha Lakshmi and I have moved from being antagonists to being close friends. It took some time for me to be able to accept the idea of money as living currency. There's nothing wrong with having a few dollars in reserve to help with hard times. In fact, now I follow the advice given by Suze Orman on CNBC to make certain we have an adequate emergency fund.

I wish the woman who loved limos could trade her sense of unworthiness in for a turning of the wheel in the cleaning division of the zendo she decided to leave. There's nothing quite like getting down on your hands and knees and scrubbing floors as well as sinks and toilets. Cleaning is a great way to cut through the grease of pretension.

For my first seva ever, I cleaned rooms with three other women to get them ready for summer. In addition to Anglo-Saxon me, one women was Italian, one Armenian, one Japanese. We worked hard all weekend long. I saw one of these women not long ago at a chanting of "The Guru Gita" in New York City's Central Park. She did not recognize me now that I have taken *sannyas,* but I felt the sweet glow of her smile recalling the seva we offered, side by side, to create a place of refuge for visiting seekers, students, and disciples.

When Gurus sense fraudulence, they can make more trouble than disciples care to remember, at least prior to the dawning of spiritual maturity. I, for one, am immensely grateful for all the troublemaking activities I have had the good sense to perceive, or be shown outright.

Without the troublemaking function of Gurus, devotees might fall asleep as Jesus's disciples did in the Garden of Gethsemane on the eve of his death.

CHAPTER IV

The One Unpardonable 'Sin,' Denial of the Holy Ghost

In addition to alluding directly to Jesus's omniscient powers—"And Jesus knew their thoughts"—Matthew 12 opens the spiritual house to one of the most startling claims in the whole of Christianity, a major spiritual truth which too often lies submerged. In verses 31 and 32 of the King James version of the *Holy Bible*, Jesus speaks:

> Wherefore I say unto you, All manner of sin and blasphemy shall be forgiven unto men: but the blasphemy *against* the Holy Ghost shall not be forgiven unto men.
>
> And whosoever speaketh a word against the Son of man, it shall be forgiven him: but whosoever speaketh against the Holy Ghost, it shall not be forgiven him, neither in this world, neither in the *world* to come.

In other words, the one unpardonable error lies in denial of the Holy Ghost. Declining to acknowledge the living power is the worst kind of insult. The one sin which cannot be forgiven is the refusal to work with the Holy Spirit, known as Ruach Hakodesh in mystical Judaism, as Maha Kundalini Shakti in the Indian religions, and as Windhorse fueled by Tummo, or intense heat, in Buddhism.

Why did Jesus speak in such strong terms about the power of the Holy Ghost? At the risk of repetition, it must be said emphatically: *the Holy Ghost is the Enlightener.* Jesus, Shaktipat Guru, knew how to awaken the sacred power and turn up the heat as needed. With the Holy Ghost still sleeping there can be little movement toward salvation, or *moksha*, as the state of liberation is known in Hinduism, Yoga, and the Hindu Tantra. Preparatory work can be done if one is living a good life, and goodness is vitally important, but the royal road to liberation begins to be paved when Maha Kundalini Shakti comes awake.

One of the best and most accessible introductions to how "the sacred power" works can be found in Swami Kripananda's book by the same name. This elegant text is a must on any Holy Spirit reading list. Likewise, Lilian Silburn's book entitled *Kundalini: The Energy of the Depths* delves into different awakenings and their degrees of intensity as does Dr. Joan Harrigan's *Kundalini Vidya.*

While the New Testament is ripe with references to the Holy Spirit, no such systematic guides exist for Christians. More so than other religions, Indian spiritual systems have developed the study of Maha Kundalini Shakti into a science. At least in terms of the passage of Maha Kundalini Shakti through the chakras, the path from awakening to *moksha* is well-marked. This path is not always kindly received by Christians who do not understand that there is no difference between the Holy Spirit and Maha Kundalini Shakti.

The Holy Spirit is a visible presence in the Black Church in America—far more so than in predominantly White churches more intent on doctrine than spontaneous reception of the power. In African-American churches, the Spirit moves largely in response to sound through the rousing and rhythmic music offered in praise of the Lord. In terms of the greater freedom afforded to the Holy Spirit, Black and Pentecostal Churches have more in common with each other and with certain Asian paths than with conventional Christianity.

Unlike mainstream Christians, Pentecostals are encouraged to experience the Holy Spirit in congregational settings. In fact, a Charismatic movement emerged in North America in the 1960s which adopted Pentecostal beliefs and practices. The movement has drawn both support and criticism.

"Hindu Gurus and Pentecostal Preachers Are Identical," a website on the Internet, draws precise correspondences between Maha Kundalini Shakti and the Holy Spirit. Interestingly, renewed interest in Charismatic Christianity began to occur about the time a number of Indian and Tibetan Gurus began arriving in the Western hemisphere.

The Holy Spirit began to move in different cultural groups simultaneously. A burst of Shakti occurred in consciousness which resulted in an outpouring of the sacred power. Perhaps the 1960s, 70s, 80s, and 90s will someday be known as the Great Holy Spirit Awakening.

The Toronto Blessing is one such Charismatic group which has attracted considerable notice. The Blessing began in January 1994 at the Toronto Airport Vineyard Church when John and Carol Arnott called in Rev. Randy Clark, who was influenced by Rodney Howard Browne, a South African preacher, to conduct a revival. The Toronto Blessing has become well-known for its ecstatic worship, including what is known as "falling or resting in the Spirit."

Laughter, shaking and crying, and roaring like animals are documented instances of the Holy Spirit moving through the congregation of the Toronto Blessing, also known as the Toronto Airport Christian Fellowship (TACF). Rodney Howard Browne is known for being a major "Firestarter" in the Pentecostal movement, and his presence at the Toronto Blessing helped to impart the spirit of intoxication and laughter for which the movement is known. These manifestations of the Holy Spirit are not terribly different from those described in Yoga as *kriyas.* They should be familiar to most anyone who has experienced a Shaktipat retreat, a Kriya Yoga gathering, or possibly worked with a therapist who is a member of the Kundalini Research Network.

Pentecostal ministers John and Carol Arnott founded an organization and website called, "Catch the Fire." Appropriately named, "Catch the Fire" could also be the name of a Kundalini Yoga group, a text devoted to Kundalini process, or an advertisement for a breath work session conducted by Stanislaus and Christina Grof. When the fire starts to roar, those who catch the spirit often cannot help but experience what are known as Yogic *kriyas*, or movements of the body, signaling purification.

An estimated 279 million Pentecostals worldwide trace their origins to the early 20th century Azusa Street Revival in Los Angeles which sources say resulted in the spread of Pentecostalism throughout the United States. Since the 1960s, Pentecostalism has grown to an approximate 500 million followers involved in the Pentecostal and Charismatic wings of Christianity.

Pentecostals who are baptized with the Holy Spirit tend to see their movement as reflecting the same kind of spiritual power and teachings found in the Apostolic age of the early Christian church after Pentecost. This is an important observation. It underscores the message found in Matthew 12:31-32 advising Christians of the central role the Holy Spirit plays in the work of salvation.

In the Eastern Orthodox Church, the Christian becomes more wholly unified with Christ through the fire of God's love in the action of the Holy Spirit. Born in God's image, each person is called to *theosis,* fulfillment of one's likeness to God, or of one's divinity. The Holy Spirit serves as both author and guardian of the scriptures, thus strengthening the bond between Christians and the mystical body of Christ.

Unlike Pentecostal Christians, Buddhists usually conduct their work of purification in secret. At the level of the *Vajrayana*, many take vows to their Gurus and Lamas as they continue the process of working with Windhorse and Tummo. Kabbalists in the postmodern West are finding their way out of secrecy and into public venues. No less a celebrity than the rock star Madonna is a student of the Kabbalah. In Islam, the *Quran* does not recognize a distinct energy known as the Holy Spirit. To do so would be offensive to most traditional Muslims who place their faith in Allah, the one and only God.

However, Islam has a mystical wing known as Sufism. Sufi dervishes whirl with the sacred power into ecstasy. What printed texts are necessary when whirling mimics the motion of Maha Kundalini Shakti, recognized by some Sufis as the name of the holy energy? Good commentaries on Sufi initiation and process can be found in the work of Ireena Tweedy and her student Llewellyn Vaughan-Lee who has emerged as a major Sufi teacher headquartered in northern California.

Unlike his Indian feminine counterpart, Maha Kundalini Shakti, the Holy Ghost was assigned a male gender in Christianity as the church became increasingly patriarchal. We could say Maha Kundalini and the Holy Ghost are the Shakti and Shiva of the world's religions, but they are one and the same power, so their gender designations are more cultural than theological.

According to Christian scriptures, the Holy Spirit is one with the Father and the Son. Thus, some mainstream Christians blend the Holy Spirit into the Trinity without paying much attention to his individual power. This blending may be one way in which the power of the Spirit is unintentionally diminished. In fact, the power of the Holy Spirit needs to be recognized and nurtured. She will do the work for women as well as men, but her grace must be fueled by human willingness (or *iccha shakti*) to address the sins, or habitual patterns as Ani Pema Chodron would have it, which keep us stuck in selfishness—the major block to liberation.

According to J.J. Hurtak, the Christian church's "new response" to the "image of the Holy Spirit" is to try and be more sensitive to her feminine dimensions. A quiet revolution is taking place in Christian circles, Hurtak says, largely as a result of new findings in the Dead Sea scriptures, the *Coptic Nag Hammadi*, and Jewish mystical texts written concurrently with early Christian scriptures.

The church's willingness to regard the Holy Spirit as feminine may also result from the not-so-quiet pressure applied by feminist critics such as Mary Daly whose *Beyond God the Father* created openings for other feminist theologians to ask germinal questions. Additionally, the importation of Eastern religions into the Western hemisphere from the 1960s forward has helped to place feminine images of the Holy Spirit on the theological map. These two historical developments may be inter-related as a result of feminist women leaving the Christian church in search of communities in which they feel they can grow spiritually instead of being treated as second-class citizens. Indigenous and pagan groups have tended to attract women seeking greater freedom in spiritual matters.

The Holy Spirit has a feminine dimension in Judaism known as Shekinah, but she was co-opted by patriarchs who became overly invested in institutional politics. Contemporary Judaism may be in the process of re-discovering Shekinah. Christianity, too, stands to gain some of the intuitive power it surrendered to the masculine logos, especially during the time of the Crusades, by re-realigning with the power of Shekinah inherent in its Jewish parent.

The sacred feminine is making herself felt in work ranging from the pioneering scholarship of Rosemary Radford Ruether to the bold and rule-breaking ministry of Nadia Bolz-Weber, author of *Pastrix*. The Spirit in her feminine form can be wild. She isn't always welcome in polite churches.

Be gender identifications as they may be, Jesus called sinning against the Holy Ghost unpardonable, so it may help to examine the gender-neutral word "sin." Sin actually derives from the Latin *synne*, meaning "to miss one's mark." The term comes from archery. Greek and Hebrew translations for sin render a similar meaning. Unfortunately, in some Christian circles, the concept of sin has become an Augustinian cousin to total depravity. Thinking ill of ourselves can obscure habitual patterns from being seen clearly as well as feed a sense of unworthiness. If we think of ourselves as fallen angels, it may be more difficult to see and accept the sacred power as an energy living inside us as well as in the hands and heart of the Master Teacher, Jesus. Unworthiness, like selfishness, is an obstacle to liberation.

In speaking about the gifts of the Holy Spirit, how many Christians have we known who claim: "Oh, not me, I'm unworthy"? This sense of unworthiness tends to extend into many areas of life. When "not good enough" weaves its way through the fabric of who we are, then it becomes very difficult for us to see ourselves as good candidates for spiritual growth—much less as beings who are capable of attaining the same state as the Christ.

Mainstream Christianity would benefit by placing greater emphasis on the Holy Spirit as a living, breathing entity. Many postmodern Christian commentators speak of the unifying power of the sacred energy but fail to mention her power to purify human beings internally. A well-known Episcopal bishop calls her a "sign" of God's grace. She is far more than sign or symbol. She is Grace in action.

A number of years ago, I participated in an extended retreat at a spiritual center located in the northeastern United States. Early in the retreat, the teaching monks asked us to write a paragraph defining the Holy Spirit and how we perceived the spirit in our lives.

Having been strongly influenced by the work of Henri Bergson and Teilhard de Chardin, I wrote confidently, "The Holy Spirit is a metaphor for the universal energy at the center of the universe."

The next day, a teacher leading the morning session said, the Holy Spirit isn't just a metaphor.

I was stunned. If not a metaphor for the "force that through the green fuse drives the flower," as the Irish poet Dylan Thomas wrote, then what in the world could the spirit be?

Later in the retreat, I approached one of the teaching monks about the pressure I was feeling. It felt like fingers of fire were pushing through tissues, an electrical force cracking bones in my head.

It bothers some people, the monk said. It doesn't bother others.

What should I do? I wondered. I had never felt

anything quite like the vibrations circulating inside my body.

The monk told me to keep things simple and practical. He emphasized the word practical, which was good for me as a *jnana yogi* whose immediate inclination was to go in search of every book published on the subject of the Holy Spirit and begin plundering the pages.

Experience of the Holy Spirit, alias Maha Kundalini Shakti or Windhorse, is the great teacher. Knowledge obtained from books helps us to understand how the spirit works, but ultimately, we must sense her movement in our bodies, feel her current in our minds, and recognize her presence deep in our hearts. It is she who stitches the threads connecting us to the mystical body of Christ, otherwise known as the Jagadguru.

The influence of both Hindu and Buddhist Tantra in the West has been immensely helpful in postmodern times, as have certain forms of psychotherapy, in assisting people to dissolve crippling internal judgments. Judgment, unfortunately, can reinforce habitual patterns such as rebellion against the truths of the religion in which we are raised.

If *moksha*, enlightenment, or Heaven, is the mark, then it is essential to awaken the Holy Ghost. The surest and safest way to ignite the sacred power is to receive Shaktipat from a Shaktipat Guru, a Buddhist Lama, a mystical Jewish rabbi, or a Christian or Interfaith minister who knows how to work with the Holy Spirit.

A good Kabbalist is hard to find, but some are beginning to teach in venues such as the Kripalu and Omega Institutes. It is relatively easy to locate Hasidic rabbis in Brooklyn. Some still conduct summer camps in the Catskill Mountains not far from Karma Triyana Dharmachakra, a Buddhist monastery near Woodstock, NY.

The Holy Spirit seems to move in and out of various geographic locales, but she remains constant when it comes to insisting on recognition. She likes to be seen and praised. As Jesus knew so well—hence warned his flock—she is necessary to salvation.

CHAPTER V

Importance of Discipline, Ethics, and Emptying

Virtually all religions contain a code of ethics for discipline in living. These codes are informed by the centrality of love or compassion as a guiding force. Just as The Ten Commandments offer an ethical system for Jewish people and Christians, so *The Bhagavad Gita* offers a yoga of discipline for Hindus and yogis. The eight-fold path of Buddhism and the precepts also offer a splendid code for ethical living. Good commentaries on virtually all these codes of ethics are available in different languages.

It is, indeed, useful when working with the Holy Spirit to live a life of discipline. The Holy Spirit can do the work of purification more quickly if spiritual seekers live in a disciplined fashion. If the Holy Spirit encounters internal obstacles, she can be relentless. After all, purification is her job. To some, Buddhism is thought to be value-neutral, but Shambhala Buddhism offers a "well-lit path" to counter the effects of a wild ride aboard Windhorse. The Pentecostals say that certain conditions, if present in a believer's life, could cause delay in receiving the baptism of the Holy Spirit. For Pentecostals, these conditions include weak faith, unholy living, imperfect consecration, and egocentric motives.

When I returned to Kentucky from nearly two decades of life in the snowbelt of northwestern Pennsylvania, I sat for a period of some eleven years with the Shambhala Buddhists in Lexington, KY. Tantric in orientation, Shambhala Buddhism is very close philosophically to Kashmir Shaivism, my anchor path.

I wanted to learn Buddhism from the inside out, so I completed the Sacred Warrior path and am, in fact, a registered Shambhala Guide in addition to being an ordained Interfaith minister and a member of the Saraswati order of monastics. I have taken courses at Shambhala Mountain Center in the Colorado Rockies, and my Warrior Assembly program was held at Karma Choling in Barnet, Vermont, under the able direction of Acharya John Rockwell. Also, I have taught courses for the Bernard Osher Foundation for senior learners hosted by the Shambhala Center in Lexington. The Shambhala *sangha* is wonderfully generous and filled with intelligent people, many of whom are distinguished in their chosen professions.

Shambhala is a very good path for people who feel they need to be directed from one rung of the spiritual ladder to the next. The road signs are clearly marked, and Shambhala trains capable teachers to assist students on their spiritual journey. Like most paths, Shambhala understandably does not emphasize its similarities to other spiritual systems. Windhorse, for instance, is not talked about as an analogue to Maha Kundalini Shakti or the Holy Spirit.

One day, a senior student of Shambhala cautioned me about the potential dangers of Kundalini awakening. During the course of our conversation, I thought, "Someone needs to set up an Interspiritual umbrella structure to help seekers in an age of religious plurality negotiate seemingly different ideas contained in religious systems which are, in actuality, the same."

Such an Interspiritual structure could be immensely helpful to students and program administrators. When students move from one path to another, they are sometimes at odds as to the best course of study given their previous training and experience. Administrators sometimes tell such students to start at the most basic level when their knowledge is significantly more advanced.

Of course, it never hurts for students to begin at Level 1 of any given path and learn the discourse of a particular tradition as I did with Shambhala Buddhism. The teachings and concepts may be similar among the traditions, but they invariably have different names and the contexts in which they are presented differ. In the age of Interspirituality, it is important to honor and preserve difference.

Participation in courses in different spiritual orientations is a great way to enhance intellectual discipline. While continuing to empty out unnecessary patterns of thought and feeling, students can benefit from intra-spiritual work by renewing their acquaintance with humility. Defined as the ability to say, "I don't know," humility helps spiritual seekers to stay intellectually and spiritually honest. Humility can be seen as a Christian analogue to Zen Buddhist beginner's mind.

Sometimes, in the midst of moving from one path to another, students get caught in discursive thinking. They confuse mental chatter with genuine intellectuality. When that happens, it may be time to meditate. As Sakyong Mipham Rinpoche, head of Shambhala, suggests, it takes courage to take one's seat on the meditation cushion.

As L.M. Richardson writes in his online lessons, underscoring the dangers of discursive thinking, Jesus's gift of the Holy Spirit is "not an abstract concept." Further, the Holy Spirit can be heard as well as seen, and the flowing of her heat can be felt and sensed, no matter the religious affiliation.

Richardson continues to discuss practices used by early Christians to fuel the Holy Spirit's movement.

Breathing exercises, much like Indian *pranayama*, have been traced back 1,000 years in both Eastern Orthodox and Roman Catholic monastic communities.

St. Clement, Bishop of Alexandria (150-215 CE) speaks of the Christian path as it was originally taught approximately 150 years after Jesus introduced the Holy Spirit to his followers. St. Clement laments how much of the early teachings have been lost. As Richardson notes, in the older days, the church claimed to be able to do much more than make people good for the sake of goodness alone. The church included three stages of purification.

Sometimes known as "The Stromata of St. Clement," the three stages are as follows: 1) purification—the opening of the heart and the diminishing of the ego; 2) illumination—the Holy Spirit reveals the deep things of God; 3) perfection—the soul feels the presence of infinite consciousness as its true nature.

Stage three evokes the title of a spiritual autobiography written by Peters Hayes entitled, *The Supreme Adventure: The Yoga of Perfection.* The Hayes text includes an unforgettable passage somewhat like the three levels noted in "The Stromata of St. Clement." Hayes had risen early in the morning to chant "The Guru Gita." He completed the chant "humming" internally. The humming sound of bees is a well-known characteristic of Kundalini Shakti operating in the upper chakras. The bees are representatives of infinite consciousness who come calling when a being has attained enough perfection by purification to receive their honey.

Also, it is fascinating how close the Stromata is to the Shambhala Buddhist progression from Sacred Warrior to Vajrayana practice. If "universe" is substituted for "God," "Windhorse" for "the Holy Spirit" and "luminous emptiness" for "infinite consciousness," we can see how spiritual terms from different paths can be interchangeable.

Unlike some forms of Western Christianity, Shambhala Buddhism does not accept the doctrine of original sin. In Shambhala Buddhism, human beings are seen as basically good. Everything is grist for the mill, and it is not unusual to hear Shambhalians say to newcomers, "We'll work with it," whatever "it" may be. This lack of judgment provides a spiritual setting in which practitioners generally feel accepted, rather than harshly critiqued by a wrathful deity or a less than judicious jury who might or might not help with the journey to "luminous emptiness."

A hospitable and flexible atmosphere is important in times when many spiritual seekers have received virtually no instruction from any religion, and further, do not want to be told what to do. Increasingly, such seekers are looking for congregations like the First Church of Religious Science in Atlanta which grew in the late 1970s from seven people meeting in a downtown hotel to a packed auditorium in the High Museum of Art. Founded by Ernest Holmes, Religious Science helps people clear their minds and live more effectively. For many, such help is very important and more attractive than any mythic narrative.

The Christian admonition to "Judge not that ye be not judged" (Matthew 7:1) is sometimes lost among even the most devoted Christians who believe they have a right to judge others by virtue of Christianity's status as the world's largest religion. This tendency is most unfortunate since time put into preparing sermons, cleaning the sanctuary, and showing people to their seats on Sunday mornings is helpful toward purification but does not necessarily equate with spiritual maturity.

Jesus the Christ accepted all who sought his counsel,

especially the poor and destitute who are routinely judged in "nice" churches. Declining to judge others resembles the Hindu-Buddhist notion of "right speech," and this practice helps Maha Kundalini Shakti to display the compassionate elements contained in her identity as Windhorse.

Of course, not all Shambhala Buddhists are non-judgmental all the time. Neither are yogis and yoginis who are still in spiritual process. Projecting one's own trips and "stuff" onto others is part of the movement toward liberation. It could be useful to spiritual seekers of all orientations to learn about projection as the way the mind works prior to enlightenment rather than as a right to be exercised when spiritual comrades are perceived as being different, a friend makes a hurtful remark, or a neighbor brings a cake with "bought" icing to a community dinner. As Chogyam Trungpa Rinpoche advised, it is better to say, "You honor me with your insult," than to huddle in groups complaining about perceived offenses.

In addition to Shaktipat, neo-Hindu traditions in the West frequently speak of the confusing nature of the senses and their blinding powers. Gurus often instruct their students in the cultivation of virtues. Cultivating virtues helps with purification.

For instance, a certain Indian Jagadguru was commanded by his Guru to give Shaktipat, and in so doing, he broke from the tradition of testing disciples extensively before offering *divya diksha*, or initiation. His approach was to give Shaktipat, or Kundalini awakening, in a safe setting, and let the seeds fall for those who could receive the grace-bestowing power. A fairly high degree of purification in seekers is necessary for the Shakti to come awake. In this Jagadguru's day, as in contemporary times, seekers were not always ready to receive Shaktipat. Others were prepared in varying degrees, and the Shakti responded accordingly. When awakened, Kundalini guides seekers to liberation, perhaps more quickly in disciples who enact a generous portion of "Disciple's Grace."

Jesus appears to have offered Shaktipat in a manner similar to the above Indian Jagadguru. He did not set up a school and require disciples to take a number of courses or be tested to qualify for the gift of awakening. According to John 3:17, "For God sent not his son into the world to condemn the world but that the world, through him, might be saved." *Through him* are the operative words in this passage. Jesus was a Shaktipat Guru, and by igniting the sacred energy in scholars and scoundrels alike, as did this Jagadguru, he set about transforming the world, one disciple at a time.

Sometimes, yogis on various Yogic paths are guided to teachers in other traditions. One Indian Jagadguru is said to have traveled the whole of India four times and sought out some 40 teachers in his quest for knowledge before he came reverentially to the sacred feet of his Guru who gave him the experiential knowledge he had been seeking.

If seekers are feeling frustrated and unable to "get with the program" of a spiritual path, or adjust to its code of ethics, they should feel no shame in seeking out a teacher who speaks a language they can understand. An attractive feature of the age of religious plurality, of Interspirituality, is this—many doors are open.

At the same time, there is much to be said for mining one path. Shopping for spiritual paths can be costly in terms of time and energy. If seekers feel they are growing spiritually on a given path, then why change? Even when times are hard, as they invariably will be in the course of the spiritual journey, seekers may want to ask: is the difficulty generated by the path, or have I gotten hooked on discursive thinking?

In recent years, some Christians have been turning from mainstream to Pentecostal Christianity for an experience of the Holy Spirit. The Pentecostal churches historically are known for speaking in tongues and allowing the congregation to express movements of the Holy Spirit in dramatic ways. Pentecostal Christianity is similar to Kriya Yoga. In certain yogic groups, "kriya rooms" have existed where yogis could stay while dealing with various manifestations of Maha Kundalini Shakti during the proceedings of a Shaktipat Intensive. As the groups came of age, and seekers learned to contain the Shakti, there was less need for specific spaces devoted to kriyas.

Au contraire to all this drama Hank Hanegraaf has written in a book entitled *Counterfeit Revival* in which he critiques the frenetic activities of Pentecostals and Charismatics. The fire is too "muddy" for Hanegraaf who prefers a more orderly form of worship. Hanegraaf is not alone in his objections. Mainstream Christians often consider the Holy Spirit to be too disruptive to admit into the liturgy.

Nonetheless, the early Christian church was built on the Pentecostal vision. When people asked Peter what they should do following the crucifixion and resurrection of Jesus, he said, "Repent and be baptized, every one of you, in the name of Jesus Christ, for the forgiveness of your sins; then you will receive the gift of the Holy Spirit" (Acts 2: 1-39). Thus, the clearing of ethical violations was important in early Christianity for the Holy Spirit to descend.

After the crucifixion of Jesus, his disciples were afraid. Seeing the Master resurrected reportedly relieved their misgivings. Jesus had told them to wait in Jerusalem to be baptized by the Holy Spirit. On the Jewish festival of Shavuot, or Pentecost, the disciples were gathered together when suddenly a huge wind blew through the house, and fiery tongues enflamed their hearts. They were filled with the Holy Spirit and given instructions as to how to go forth in the name of spreading the Lord's sacred energy in the world.

In some respects, Jesus the Christ embodies elements similar to Buddhism and the older Hindu tradition. Like the Buddha, Jesus insisted on an ethical basis for living. Like certain Hindu Gurus, Jesus knew how to awaken the sacred energy. Jesus connected the importance of ethical living to the necessity for receiving the Holy Spirit. In modern times, this connection is too often severed. Healing this rupture is one of the places where the Interspiritual movement can be effective as Interspirituals tend to be synthetic thinkers who have little need of defending doctrinal preferences.

In Matthew 12:27, Jesus speaks of casting out devils. Sins can get stuck in what Hindus and Yogis call the subtle body. In Roman Catholicism, this teaching has led to the practice of exorcism, a cousin to Kriya Yoga. When compared with the Eastern religions, casting out devils most likely means dissolving karma, or embedded *samskaras*, which can pack a wallop similar to demonic power. It is difficult for seekers to adhere to ethical standards when they are driven by *samskaras* which feed into habitual patterns.

Essentially, the law of karma is equivalent to the law of cause and effect, which means simply: we human beings reap what we sow (Galatians 6:6-18). If too much negative karma is stored in the subtle body, it may take an exorcist, or a Kriya Yoga specialist, to assist with its removal. More than once in the Christian Bible, Jesus chases out devils, or dissolves *samskaras*, from the subtle bodies of people who come to him in pain.

Of course, the best way to keep sins and negative karma from being stored in the subtle body is to live by a sound code of ethics. If a seeker is driven by lust, for example, honoring the adultery commandment can be difficult.

Does anyone take adultery seriously in postmodern times? Adultery appears to have lost some ground as one of the 10 Commandments. Nonetheless, adultery has a bad habit of creating lots of trouble for those who feel the need to overstep their boundaries. While adultery does not attract karma as seriously as killing, its effects need to be cleared from the subtle body. If a seeker is suffering from the karma of a breakup due to adultery, he or she might want to spend some time working with a 12 Step group or a good therapist. When negative karma is stuck in the subtle body, it can manifest as compulsive behavior as well as badgering a former partner who may have moved on to another marriage.

Jesus, no less than some Indian and Tibetan teachers, was a Guru who understood how to work with karma. He took the shortcomings of his disciples to heart, and in the end, he gave his life to free human beings from the forces which can cause excruciating pain. In the final analysis, there is nothing to get free from except our own selfishness, especially prevalent in the West where a pronounced collective *ahamkara,* or ego, prevails. If placed at the center of home and society, a good code of ethics composed of teachings across the spiritual traditions could go a long way toward uprooting self-centeredness.

I live in a part of the world where there has been considerable controversy over whether or not The 10

Commandments ought to be posted in public spaces. Finally, the Supreme Court ruled the Commandments could be displayed in public so long as ethical injunctions from other religions were allowed as well.

It is easy to imagine The 10 Commandments hanging beside the Five Precepts of Buddhism, but such has yet to happen in the courthouse of Pulaski Co., Kentucky with its 92 Baptist churches. At Slate Branch Ashram, the Shiva Nataraj hangs next to the 23rd Psalm above the Master Teachers wall, and The Five Teachings of Adishraddha, or Sacred Feet Yoga, are displayed in Shraddha Loka, our meditation hall. Although the Five Teachings are Interspiritual, or Intra-Tantric, in nature, The First Teachings are a recasting of the *Mahavakya*, or great command from Jesus, to love our neighbors *as* ourselves. In our quarterly retreats, we emphasize *as* in the First Teachings. As Ani Pema Chodron has noted, there are many people in the United States alone who have never felt love of any kind, much less love for themselves.

In postmodern times, being good seems to be increasingly uninteresting. The fierce injunction to stop sinning found in early Christianity doesn't seem to be working very well for postmoderns who need to be able to see the psycho-emotional wisdom behind any set of rules. Of particular concern in postmodern times is the obsession with killing. The Command, Thou Shalt Not Kill, appears to have lost considerable clout. Although not killing is a Buddhist precept as well, and Buddhism is increasingly attractive to young seekers, we live in an age in which it is difficult to go on the Internet and not find yet another horrendous murder or shoot-out in a public space. Similarly, the percentage of killing-obsessed TV shows is astronomically high.

Why, as a society, are we so enamored of killing? Is it because the Commandment not to kill no longer prevails, so there is no rule in place to inveigh against taking the life of another human being? Is it because the Freudian super-ego may be disappearing as civilization grows increasingly discontent? Are we becoming a world of sociopaths who must have ever more intense forms of entertainment to keep from being bored?

In December of 2013, the story of a newlywed couple who killed a man and then went to a strip club circulated on the Internet. The couple allegedly lured the man on Craig's List, and when they got him in their car, the husband strangled him from behind, and the wife stabbed him twenty times. They had killed for the thrill of it, the husband admitted freely.

Would this kind of killing be happening if we lived in a society with a strong sense of ethical values? Like ancient Rome, we are weakened by our extravagant indulgence in sense pleasures. Like ancient Rome, we have too much debt—read karma—and our credit is over-extended. Like ancient Rome, we are quite capable of trying another Jesus for treason.

Some people think of Maha Kundalini Shakti, or the Holy Spirit, as being value-neutral, but unethical actions actually block her movement. In some cases, like the senseless killing described above, karma will have to be burned off before this young couple has any hope of being rehabilitated. If they go to jail—and who knows what the verdict will be if they manage to hire an effective defense attorney?—what are their chances of finding their way to a saner way of thinking about their fellow human beings? If they are released from prison, will they kill again?

It is good when our prison systems teach meditation

in conjunction with ethical values rather than stashing the incarcerated in solitary cells to fend for themselves. In cases as serious as the couple who killed, they probably do not have the resources to save themselves from themselves. If given the opportunity, Maha Kundalini Shakti can act as a blast furnace, burning up karma quickly and putting people in touch with better parts of themselves, but she must be awake to spark the fires of purification.

In my work with seekers in Kundalini process, I have come to see the inculcation of a strong sense of ethics as essential. Sometimes, students tend to think of lying as just another form of public relations, and stealing is okay if you get what you want and don't get caught. Spicing up primary relationships with fantasies about other lovers is hardly adulterous—it helps to keep the primary relationship in place. So what if a partner senses your thoughts are elsewhere? It does no good for students to spend their hard earned money on Kundalini work and then sabotage their process by behaving in unethical ways. If I don't catch them, Maha Kundalini Shakti will and then write their names in what Christians call the "Book of Life."

Maha Kundalini Shakti is the same as the Guru. The Holy Spirit is the same as Jesus the Christ. Windhorse is the same as the Rinpoche or Lama. The "Book of Life" is the same as the Subtle Body on which karmic imprints are indelibly recorded. Interspiritually, there is no difference between the Holy Spirit and the Master Teacher.

The sacred energy is extremely intelligent, and she knows exactly where to work to free us from the baggage we carry. If we cooperate by doing self-analysis, a time-honored practice in Yoga, and working with rather than against the Shakti, we can move faster along the rungs of the ladder than we might otherwise. The goal, of course, is ultimate happiness, heaven, or consciousness emptied of "sin" and accumulated karma.

It may be difficult for us to have compassion toward the couple who killed for the thrill of it. They may seem like enemies of society. But, Jesus instructed us to love our enemies as well as our neighbors. We can help by holding them in consciousness and sending strength for them to clean up their karma.

The narrative of how Jesus died for our sins continues to be at the core of many Christian sermons. It is a powerful message. A similar claim exists in neo-Hinduism in which the Guru is said to remove disciples' karma much as Jesus takes away sins. If the story of Jesus's death is allowed to diminish individual willingness to grow stronger ethically, however, it loses some of its effectiveness.

If Jesus is our Guru, we must help him. We must be willing to take a serious look at who we are internally, at the materials we have stashed in our beggars' bowls, and try not to pass the spiritual buck by saying Jesus will do the work for us.

Ultimately, as Cynthia Bourgeault suggests, Jesus was a Tantric Master. He showed us how to empty out (Philippians 2:7). In the process of emptying out the karma accumulated in our bowls, we become "luminously empty," to employ Tibetan Buddhist terminology for the Kenotic process.

Moreover, in Matthew 12:30, Jesus says, " . . . he that gathereth not with me scattereth abroad." This verse is particularly interesting, because the language resembles diction used in the contemporary Hindu Tantra. She who "gathereth not" the Shakti "scattereth" the sacred energy in ways which are not useful to spiritual growth. She can waste the gift of Shaktipat after it has been bestowed by disregarding the ethical life. He that "gathereth not" the seed of creation "scattereth" the sacred energy in pools of darkness. Keeping the focus may be hard in an age in which there are so many distractions, but it can mean the difference between misery and bliss.

Therefore, it is good to live mindfully and ethically, taking care of the body and heart as well while actively engaged in spiritual process. It has as much to do with life, breath, and en-lightenment as with sin and *samskaras*.

CHAPTER VI

Zechariah's Golden Lampstand

Where did Jesus learn how to give Shaktipat? Was Jesus, like Bhagawan Nityananda, an *avadhut*, a Master who arrived on earth already enlightened? Did he travel to India on the trade routes where he learned about Shaktipat initiation from India Gurus? Or, did he encounter Jewish rabbis who knew about the workings of the Spirit from studying the Kabbalah?

There is no way to know for certain whether or not Jesus was born an avadhut. *Avadhuts* are the rarest beings on earth. They need no instruction. They come onto the earth plane usually in mysterious ways, prepared to teach, sometimes as much through silence as by way of sermons and *dharma* talks.

More information about the 18-year period in which Jesus went missing might help to resolve the question as to where Jesus learned how to give Shaktipat. Different theories exist. Jesus could have trained with a teacher in the desert, possibly in an Essene community near the Dead Sea, and returned to Jerusalem to give Shaktipat after he had received instruction. When he began to preach and heal, he clearly functioned at the level of a Shaktipat Guru.

As recounted in the *Holy Bible*, wise men were dispatched at the time of Jesus's birth to verify his status as a savior—an event which argues for Jesus as an *avadhut*, or possibly a *bodhisattva*. This practice is not unlike Buddhist Lamas being sent to determine whether or not a child is a reincarnation of a Rinpoche. In fact, Jesus may have been a reincarnation of a Rinpoche or Guru. Especially if we take seriously the Indo-Tibetan theories related to the missing years, the wise men can be seen as Lamas who were sent to the Holy Land to verify the birth of another high Lama or Rinpoche.

As mentioned earlier, Jesus was found in earnest dialogue with Jewish priests while he was still a boy. The Jewish elders apparently were confounded by Jesus's wisdom. The second chapter of Luke does not disclose the subject matter being discussed. Were they trained in the Kabbalah, the rabbis most likely would not have instructed Jesus in the Sephiroth, or ten points of light, while seated in the Temple in plain view. If the Kabbalah existed at this time, and it very well could have, it may have been taught in hush-hush tones under the radar of traditional Jews—or in code. Rabbis who were secretly friendly with the Essenes, perhaps, could have given the young boy instructions as to where to go next to enhance his training.

Some scholars and students of the Kabbalah think of mystical Judaism as being an entity distinct from the *Torah* and traditional Judaism. The two are different in the emphasis mystical Judaism places on the workings of Ruach Hakodesh, or the Holy Spirit. At the same time, however, the prophets of the Old Testament knew about the "light" depicted as the Sephirot. The books of Zechariah and Ezekiel contain descriptions not unlike those of Maha Kundalini Shakti in the *Kundalini Tantra.*

As described in the book of Zechariah, the system through which Ruach Hakodesh (or Maha Kundalini Shakti) rises compares favorably to the Tree of Life in the Kabbalah and to the Indian Chakra system. In Zechariah 4:2, the prophet sees a lampstand all of gold (the *Sushumna Nadi*) with a bowl at the top (the *Keter* or the *Sahasrara Chakra*). On the golden lampstand are "seven lamps with their tubes" (seven of the ten points of light from The Tree of Life or the chakras from *Muladhara* up to *Sahasrara*).

Four of the seven lamps appear in the book of Ezekiel as wheels of light. The chakras, which come somewhat late in the Shaktipat system, according to Dr. Paul Muller Ortega, also are frequently discussed as wheels, or energy vortexes. According to Ezekiel 1:16, "The appearance of the wheels and their work was like unto the color of beryl: and they four had one likeness: and their appearance and their work was as it were a wheel in the middle of a wheel."

Ezekiel 1:22 paints a vivid picture of the seventh chakra, the *Sahasrara* or *Keter*. "Upon the heads of the living creature," according to Ezekiel, "was the color of the terrible crystal, stretched forth over their heads above." The *Keter*, or crown from the Kabbalah, is described as the divine will to create infinite light. The *Sahasrara* has 1,000 petals and is often envisioned as a crystal, or a lotus.

As L.M. Richardson writes: "It is obvious to me that it was the different colors of the wheels of light and different vibrations of the Holy Spirit located within the centers of consciousness in his own spiritual body that Ezekiel experienced with his visions of light and sound."

Although Ezekiel was writing a country removed from the home of Maha Kundalini Shakti, he saw into the subtle body and the energy vortexes. Ezekiel lived long before the birth of Jesus who could have spent the so-called "missing years" studying with Kundalini Gurus in India, or possibly other parts of Asia. Jesus's knowledge of Ruach Hakodesh or Maha Kundalini Shakti as the power which "regenerates" (John 3:5-6) suggests he could have been taught by Indian Gurus, or perhaps, by Tibetan Lamas.

Furthermore, Jesus uses language in a major passage of Ephesians similar to that found in Indian descriptions of Maha Kundalini Shakti. "Be not drunk with wine, wherein is excess; but be filled with the Spirit,"—these instructions are attributed to Jesus in Ephesians 5:18. They could well have derived from the teachings of an Indian Guru. In Indian thought, as well as in Sufism, intoxication is frequently employed as a metaphor for spiritual illumination.

The Jesus-in-India theory was first advanced in modern times by Nicolas Notovich (1894). Subsequently, several writers have made similar claims about Jesus in India: Miza Ghulam Ahmad (1899); Levi H. Lowling (1908); Sw. Abhedananda (1922); Nicholas Roerich (1923); Mathilde Ludendorff (1930); Elizabeth Claire Prophet (1956); and Holger Kersten (1982, 2001).

Nicolas Notovich, the notorious originator of the Jesus-in-India theory, reportedly visited a monastery in Ladakh where he learned of the "Life of Issa, Best of the Sons of Men." Issa is Arabic for Jesus. Notovich examined the Issa manuscript, as the story goes, and published his translation of the "Life of Saint Issa" in French in 1894. Controversy erupted immediately.

In 1922, after initially doubting the findings of Notovich, Sw. Abhedananda, a disciple of the great Bengali saint Ramakrishna, and a friend of the famous Orientalist Max Muller, re-investigated Notovich's claim. Allegedly, he was shown a manuscript championing Notovich's views. After thorough investigation, Sw. Abhedananda's opinion tended to be more sympathetic.

Following from the work of Barnett Hillman Streeter, an Oxford New Testament scholar, Elmar Gruber and Holger Kersten argued for the substantial influence of Buddhism on the teachings of Jesus. Jesus was influenced by Theravada Buddhists living in Judea, they claimed. As early as the 1930s, Streeter made a case for the ethical teachings of the Buddha bearing remarkable similarities to the Sermon on the Mount.

After Sw. Abhedananda's work, Western scholars have not been the only ones to advance the idea of Jesus's Indianess. No less an Indian Jagadguru than Paramahansa Yogananda, mentioned previously, published a two-volume work entitled *The Second Coming of Christ.* Indeed, understanding the hidden teachings of the Gospels, the intention of Yogananda's work, helps to deepen knowledge of Jesus's power as a Shaktipat Guru. Since India is the birthplace of Shakti and Shaktipat, Yogananda does not cast doubt on Jesus studying there. Yogananda's analysis of the Christ reflects a special connection to Jesus, possibly because both were Shaktipat Gurus.

Jesus in relation to India is a subject which seemingly will not die. Whether or not he actually learned about Maha Kundalini Shakti in India, however, remains open to verification by more solid evidence. Some say Notovich never visited Hemis monastery. In his text entitled *Famous Biblical Hoaxes*, Edgar J. Goodsped claims the head of Hemis monastery where Notovich discovered the Issa manuscript signed a document denouncing Notovich as a liar.

If Jesus did not travel to India, as did St. Thomas, he certainly could have had contact with Kabbalists in or near Jerusalem who understood the workings of the Holy Spirit as deeply as Indian Gurus do. Jesus may well have learned about the Holy Spirit in the form of the Sephiroth from Kabbalists who taught him secretly—or from Jewish rabbis who kept their esoteric knowledge well-contained.

Knowledge set forth in the first five books of the Old Testament, or what Jews call the *Torah*, begs the question: did Jesus need to travel to India to learn about

Maha Kundalini Shakti when information about the Holy Spirit was available in his own culture? The precise origins of his knowledge remain in question, but in practical terms, although travel in Jesus's day was hard, the trade routes were well-delineated. He may well have traveled to India and then over the Himalayas into Tibet.

In the Christian Bible, the most prominent metaphor for the Holy Spirit is the dove. Interestingly enough, in addition to being seen as a flying horse, the sacred energy appears in Shambhala Buddhism as a pigeon. Dove and pigeon are of the same family of birds, but is the metaphor strong enough to draw inferences with regard to the training of Jesus?

Interspiritual or Intra-Tantric truths have uncanny ways of transcending geographic boundaries. For those 18 missing years, Jesus may have been encamped in an Essene community near the Dead Sea. The Essenes were a mystery cult who likely knew about the sacred energy. Their teachings include work on mirroring which resembles some of the teachings from Kashmir Shaivism. In fact, the *Mahavakya,* or great statement of Jesus which instructs us to love our neighbors as ourselves is an instruction in mirroring. If we do not love ourselves, it is highly unlikely we will be able to love others, since the mirror will be clouded.

John the Baptist emerged from the wilderness with some astounding news: One far greater than he was about to appear. He was speaking of Jesus. In the language of modern Yogic communities, John was doing "advance work" for the Guru who would follow. Some scholars think John the Baptist was an Essene. If so, he and Jesus could have emerged from an Essene community to try and infuse conventional Judaism with new life. John could have traveled with Jesus to India and Tibet as his personal assistant, but we do not know where John and Jesus were prior to the time when both began to preach.

At this point in time, the question will have to remain open as to where Jesus learned how to give Shaktipat. In the midst of scholarly uncertainty, that he knew how is the more conclusive claim. If he were, indeed, an *avadhut*, he would have had no need for instruction from human teachers. Like Bhagawan Nityananda, he could have arrived on earth with all the wisdom he needed already stored in his subtle body.

Certainly, Jesus had experience of Zechariah's golden lampstand, or the chakra system from *Muladhara* to *Sahasrara* by way of a central channel, or *nadi*. He instructed others to seek the Kingdom of Heaven "within" and to climb up the ladder leading to Heaven and stabilization in the *Sahasrara*. How could he not have known Zechariah's lamp to be the channel, or ladder, by which souls come to know *Santosha*, or lasting contentment? Jesus was one who walked the earth with seven stars in his right hand (Revelation 2:1) and an undeniable radiance inscribed on his brow.

Anyone who has spent time absorbing knowledge in the presence of a Jagadguru stands to recognize similarities between the chakra system and the golden lampstand, both metaphors of illumination. Further, the highest consciousness in Yoga is sometimes out pictured as a blue star.

Only the language is different. Essentially, "Heaven" and the 1,000-petaled lotus are the same. To reach this elevated state of consciousness, all souls must ascend the ladder, gradually shedding the "sins" or *samskaras* which block the Holy Spirit from moving into the higher reaches of Dante's Paradise.

Shortly before my spiritual journey began in earnest, I was standing in my apartment in Atlanta one day when suddenly I heard a crash. Heading toward the sound, I discovered a chandelier resembling the *sahasrara* lying in bits on the dining room floor. It had fallen from the ceiling and split into tiny pieces. As the French poet Charles Baudelaire once said, we live in a "forest of symbols." The symbol of the chandelier-*sahasrara* crashing into my life has guided my spiritual journey for nearly 40 years.

A gorgeous crystal chandelier hangs in the meditation hall of my Guru's ashram. Often, when I attended meditation retreats, I looked to the light of this chandelier for inspiration. I never doubted the Yogic promise. Someday, my consciousness would sparkle with a similar radiance. Someday, I would know how it felt to live inside the "crystal"—not so "terrible," in my view, but nonetheless, the golden globe to Zechariah's stand.

In contemplating Jesus as a Jagadguru, the Master Teacher of my youth, I like to think we have come full circle. The chandelier descended and cracked only to be assembled again in terms of what William Blake called a "higher innocence." According to the British poet-prophet, human beings move from innocence through experience to innocence much like a child's. On the other side of experience, however, we take responsibility for our actions and help others do likewise.

The *Sahasrara* is the last stop the Holy Spirit makes in the long journey to freedom. Here, having attained "the peace which passeth understanding," Maha Kundalini Shakti comes to rest. Here, Windhorse gladly goes to his stable atop the seven-storey mountain.

CHAPTER VII

The Time of Fruition

In Christianity, the Holy Spirit is called "the comforter" (John 14:26). During the so-called "time of fruition," however, the Spirit can kick up a fuss. Since the Holy Spirit dislikes pretension and lies, he is called "the spirit of truth" (John 16:13). He is also known as "the spirit of God" and "the spirit of the Lord." He is, in fact, the same as God, the same as Jesus, the same as the Jagadguru. The Holy Spirit is the energy of Jesus, or the Guru's *bodhichitta,* in Buddhist terms. He or she is the electricity which lights up a seeker's house, or mind, body, and heart. She is that which roots out delusions.

According to John 16:8, the Holy Spirit "convicts." She has no choice but to nail sentient beings for shortcomings which act as obstacles to the flow of heat and light. As the sacred energy travels through the nadis, or channels in the subtle, or spiritual body, she confronts the *samskaras,* or karmic imprints. If the Holy Spirit, or Maha Kundalini Shakti, meets a particularly stubborn *samskara,* she may have to spend some extra energy persuading the human ego to let go of its defenses. She will not move on until she elicits cooperation from her subjects. For this reason, virtually every religious system on earth places emphasis on the importance of "surrender."

According to Sw. Durgananda, now Sally Kempton, writing in "Moving Through the Inner Realm," Chapter 9 of *The Heart of Meditation* (republished as *Meditation for the Love of It*), the *samskaras* are lodged in different parts of the subtle system, but the bulk are in the causal body. The deep layers, or *vasanas,* are here in the causal body, and they form the tendencies that rule from within. The *vasanas* determine what Ani Pema Chodron has called the habitual patterns that prompt us to act.

In Yoga and the Hindu Tantra, Maha Kundalini Shakti "convicts" disciples as well. People who do not practice Yoga sometimes think of the ancient science as a "feel good exercise," but Yoga is far more than stretching gently to greet the sunrise at the local fitness center. The overall system of Yoga has eight limbs—see Patanjali—instead of just one featuring the body.

Historically, Hatha Yoga is the means by which spiritual aspirants prepared to receive Shaktipat. As a system, it was developed by yogis who began to move spontaneously as they experienced the energy of Maha Kundalini Shakti. Unfortunately, in the United States and Western Europe, Hatha Yoga sometimes resembles gymnastics. But, not always. Despite the claims that Hatha Yoga has suffered as a result of its intersection with capitalism, some very good teachers are instructing students in large cities as well as small towns.

For yogis who are nearing a state of *Nirbija*, or neutralized karma, the time of fruition can be intense—a difficult stage with unseen crooks and bends. It all depends upon karma, *samskaras*, and strength of the subtle body. If the subtle body has been damaged, repair work may be needed for a yogi or *tantrika* to be able to hold the heat which accompanies intense spiritual work. Buddhists sometimes refer to this capacity as the "ability to hold one's seat."

For others, regardless of religious or spiritual affiliation, the time of fruition may seem like a blip in consciousness. In such cases, the karmic imprints are light, already significantly burned in the fires of yoga.

According to Arno Clemens Gaebelein in his 1928

text entitled "An Exegetical Examination of Every New Testament Reference to the Spirit of God," a distinct difference exists between baptism by fire and baptism by water. Baptism by fire, Gaebelein claims, is reserved for the second coming of the Christ.

When viewed through the lens of Hindu-based Tantra, fire and water are one. Fire is necessary to dislodge the *samskaras,* to heat the living water and move it through the incinerator. Fire is the purifying quality of Maha Kundalini Shakti. A Jagadguru once described her ashram as unmistakably bright with the fires of Yoga.

During the time of fruition, or "fulfillment," as it is also called, spiritual seekers who have reached a certain level of attainment must account for every morsel of karma in their beggars' bowls. There may be unresolved issues with family members, and there may be past actions which call for rectification.

In Christian terms, the time of fruition may well be analogous to the "narrowing" of the path. In Matthew 7:13-14, it is written: "Enter through the narrow gate. For wide is the gate and broad is the road that leads to destruction, and many enter through it. Small is the gate and narrow the road that leads to life, and only a few find it."

Sometimes, this passage is interpreted to mean Jesus and Christianity are the only gates by which a seeker may enter onto the road to Heaven. However, it takes very good karma to come into the presence of a Shaktipat Guru. Only a relative few from the vast numbers of people on earth will find their way to the sacred feet of such a being. Fewer, still, will stay the course to freedom upon first encounter.

Furthermore, "narrow" and "small" may refer to the central channel through which the Holy Spirit passes on her way to the crown chakra. In the process of penetrating Rudra Granthi, the "eye of the needle" evoked in Luke 18:25, she dissolves karma acquired from traveling the broad road of destruction.

Dr. Joan Harrigan, a specialist in Kundalini Yoga, calls what happens during fruition a process of "unloading." A seeker at this stage is shedding not just the karma of one lifetime, but the collective karma of past lifetimes as well. Accordingly, the process of unloading may take several years to undergo. Not infrequently, during early phases of the emptying process, seekers report seeing images of past lives roll off in meditation much like images projected onto a screen.

If successfully negotiated, the time of fruition leads to enlightenment, or perfection, as enlightenment is known in the Stromata of St. Clement. The time of fruition is the stage at which many Westerners give up and try to find solace in their habitual patterns. Some voluntarily admit, "This life isn't the last one for me—I expect to have another incarnation."

Fulfillment can come on unexpectedly in the form of sudden shifts in life circumstances, or the emergence of difficult health challenges. If a seeker is working under the tutelage of a living Guru, fruition usually happens about ten to fifteen years after the Guru-Disciple relationship is initiated via the gift of Shaktipat. The classical number of years is 12. Some people who reach this stage dig their heels in and refuse to go any further. Some say, "All I want to do is live a good life; I am not interested in that weird Kundalini process." Some try to run.

Once the Holy Spirit, or Maha Kundalini Shakti, comes awake, she will stay with a seeker until she prevails. Maha is lovingly ruthless. She is extremely smart and totally benign. She "reveals Christ to us and in us" (John 16:14-15). She shows us Buddha mind. She sanctifies, empowers, and sets us free from the needs we think we must satisfy for happiness to arrive from distant provinces when, as a long time practitioner of Yoga said, happiness happens inside.

Sometimes, during the time of fruition, disciples may feel as if they are losing ground. Habitual patterns may emerge with a vengeance. Health issues may surface, or re-surface. Meditation or prayer may feel impossible. Seekers may gain or lose several pounds. Frequently, beings during fruition either bloat or shrink. The mind can become a tempest. A seeker may feel as if he or she is experiencing the untimely onset of Alzheimer's.

As seekers reach the outer rings of enlightenment, or the thought-free state where impermanence is no longer threatening, these difficult symptoms begin to clear. Behavior which may have cost a seeker a marriage, a job, or a long-term friendship is seen for what it was—one last, frantic effort of the ego, or little *ahamkara*, to stay in control. Ultimately, the ego is no match for Maha Kundalini Shakti. The little "I" is a constricted form of the great Self, and the little darling ultimately has no choice but to surrender what she believes to be her power to the great "I am."

On the other side of fruition, seekers often feel as if they live in a state of meditation all the time. Bloaters shrink; shrinkers regain enough weight to keep from looking like Uriah Heep. Life unfolds effortlessly as seekers discover lasting happiness.

And, what of the mind?

According to Father Rainero Cantalamessa in *Sober Intoxication of the Spirit*, when the human mind "receives the ineffable joy of the Holy Spirit," it "recedes and becomes divine." While such a description may not work for most

Buddhists, it is simple to substitute "filled with light" for "divine."

Even Carolyn Gimian, the rock of meditators, probably would not object to this alternate diction. At Ani Pema Chodron's 2010 retreat in California, Gimian, who was serving as Ani Pema's Meditation Instructor, suddenly broke into a hearty rendition of "This Little Light of Mine, I'm Gonna Let It Shine."

The light cannot break through if obstructed by *samskaras* and unresolved karma. It will show in patches and splotches as long as the mind is overly active. If the human unit is being assaulted by unresolved trauma, then the trauma needs to be cleared for the Holy Spirit to shine. When the mind "recedes," to use Father Cantalamessa's word, it is replaced by, or subsumed into what some call "the mind behind mind" who will do the thinking for us if we let it. Unfailingly omniscient, this "mind behind mind," or what the Yogic scriptures call "That," is none other than the Jagadguru, or Christ consciousness.

In the life of Siddhartha Gautama, the light broke through permanently as he sat under the pipal tree in Bodh Gaya. At this stage of enlightenment, there is no return to the world of ego. Once Siddhartha put Mara to rest, his only choice was to fulfill his destiny as a Jagadguru whose energy would lead thousands to take up his teachings and practices.

That Arada Kalama slipped out of the earth plane just after his disciple's attainment is, indeed, astonishing. Of course, Shaktipat Gurus have no reason to be seen as the force guiding the sacred energy to enlightenment. They need no applause or congratulations.

In the life of Jesus, a moment in fruition is recorded in Matthew 4:1: "Then was Jesus led up of the Spirit into the wilderness to be tested of the devil." The devil was to Jesus what Mara was to Siddhartha. Like Mara, the devil assaulted Jesus for 40 days and nights with temptations.

A similar process takes place in the lives of modern seekers who reach the time of fruition. Many are presented with their habitual patterns and challenged to erase them.

I know a woman who was catapulted into fruition late one summer after she had returned from a trip around the world. She was led to believe she was going to India to take *sannyas* for purposes of becoming a co-Guru. Others had been invited to become co-Gurus, too, she learned later. She wondered if the invitation was meant to say disciples at certain advanced stages are forewarned when it is time to move more deeply into the Guru's state. Or, at a certain point, disciples must undergo intense purification in order to join in the Guru's work as apostles of the Shakti.

The woman had a habit of getting into very passionate relationships. Had she taken *sannyas* shortly after fruition began, she surely would have failed to honor her vow of celibacy. She was not a bad woman, this disciple, but she was filled with a kind of undisciplined zest for life, and she fell in love easily.

As it turned out (let's call her Hannah), Hannah was propelled back to her hometown and put through an intense self-examination process designed to show her how the pattern of falling in love was initiated and then developed into an automatic pattern. Hannah had some emotional wounds as a child and young adult, and the bells and whistles of infatuation, she discovered, afforded a way to get on top of the pain. Falling in love became what psychologists might call a "reaction formation." Perhaps not surprisingly, at one point in her life, Hannah developed a pattern of drinking too much fine wine—another way to "transcend." She came to call her drinking a form of "simulated mysticism."

For Hannah, there was a moment when her Guru stepped in and whispered, Enough. As Hannah described the process, it felt as if the Guru lifted her by the nape of the neck, shook her lovingly as she might a kitten, and then proceeded to point out the wrong-headed patterns and ideas that Hannah needed to correct.

Hannah saw six different psycho-therapists. Mara moved in to try and persuade Hannah of the delectable sensations she would experience if only she would acknowledge her desire for her dermatologist, an attractive single person. Hannah resisted. She had taken a vow of celibacy. Eventually, she succumbed and began to allow herself to experience sexual feelings for her dermatologist (let's call him Dr. Carl).

Fortunately, Dr. Carl was an advanced spiritual practitioner himself, and he knew when to terminate the relationship to get the best results for Hannah's well-being. Ultimately, Hannah realized she was in the midst of a psycho-drama—a *lila* in Yogic terms—and she was able to begin unraveling past events which led her into untenable situations.

Today, Hannah and Dr. Carl are friends. Hannah doesn't blame him for being sexually abusive; she doesn't think he was. She believes he was acting out of authentic attraction; inadvertently, he helped her to achieve a Gestalt which allowed her to let go of old patterns and move on.

Ultimately, Hannah did take *sannyas*—after the Guru had put her through 12 years of *brahmacharya*, honoring a vow of celibacy. She failed once, with her dermatologist, but after that learning experience, she had no wish to enact the habitual pattern which had created such turmoil in her life. The *vasana* had been removed; the Gestalt was complete.

It is not uncommon for difficulties among modern spiritual seekers to manifest in relational matters. Hannah is not alone as one who needed to examine her pattern of using sexual energy as a way to avoid facing deeper emotional issues. When spiritual seekers develop "crushes" and constantly feel as if they must be in love with someone, it is an almost sure sign of unresolved issues asking to be addressed. The lines between sexual and spiritual dimensions are porous, so individuals should examine their own patterns carefully to determine if their motives are like Hannah's, or if their patterns have been set up differently.

Of course, falling in love easily can also be seen as the mark of a *bhakta* who is looking for ways to play out deep feelings of devotion. Such was the case with Hannah, too. While she never experienced overtly erotic feelings for her Guru, she came through the time of fruition in a spirit of deep trust. She opened to receive what the Guru had to offer; she was never tempted to turn on the Guru as some do during this intense period. Today, Hannah remains grateful for the Guru's guidance.

Relationships have to be cleared of karma before a seeker can attain enlightenment. Relationships are probably the most important factor standing in the way of liberation. People in postmodern times think relationships are bound to bring happiness, and they tend to be disappointed when relationships don't seem to measure up to their promise.

During an evening program at the height of the season with hundreds of seekers present, a very famous Guru once said that relationships are intended to break. Many were stunned. Most people think Yoga is meant to guarantee happy relationships. Over time, we come to see there comes a time on the road to letting go of everything when intimate relationships must go, too. Even when relationships are good and sustaining, they must be sacrificed when partners make their transition to etheric realms.

In Jesus's day, for better or worse, people tended to marry for keeps. Marriage was seen in more practical terms as a way to produce children. Now, it isn't unusual for people who have been married a few years to say, "Oh, well, this may not be the person who will be my partner for the rest of my life."

Are we as a postmodern society outgrowing marriage as an institution? I don't know, and far be it from me as a *sannyasin* (who had many relationships in my former life) to pronounce judgment on people who elect to divorce and re-marry, whether straight or gay. I am concerned about the accumulation of karma. Often, when people divorce, the hard feelings are such that former partners seek to avoid contact rather than create space to make amends. Too often, emotional wounds are projected onto the children involved.

Unresolved karma stands in the way of liberation. There is no better way to collect unresolved karma than to refuse to let go of hard feelings. Old karma provokes old patterns of thought and behavior. The time of fruition cannot be negotiated successfully if seekers insist on proving themselves right where old conflicts and wounds are concerned. Mara loves unresolved karma. Mara will do her best to persuade seekers to hold on fast, especially to what one friend calls her "committee's conversations" generated by dialogues she wish she had conducted with former lovers.

Whether fortunately or unfortunately, we do not

have a record of Jesus's personal relationships—or if he had any. For Jesus, unlike Siddhartha, no clear moment of enlightenment is written down in which he became the Father, or the Jagadguru. The Jesus-Jagadguru "merger" is manifested all through the New Testament, particularly in the gospel of John. Jesus acknowledges in John 17:18 having been "sent into the world," which reflects a high sense of calling. He was acutely aware of the seed to be spread and the work to be done.

"I have finished the work which you have given me to do," Jesus says in John 17:4. Was Jesus calling out to God alone, or was an unacknowledged Jagadguru who had given him Shaktipat hidden from view? Were Jesus trained by a rabbi with knowledge of the Kabbalah, then he could have been connecting at *Ajna* chakra with a Master Teacher who taught him about the Sephirot, the mystical Jewish equivalent of the chakra system.

It is difficult to know for certain. A major part of Jesus's time of fruition appears to have happened offstage during the missing years. Although we cannot say with absolute certainty, Jesus may have completed most of his *sadhana* during the lost years. There may be scrolls still to be unearthed which will tell us more about the 15- 18 years unaccounted for in the Christian Bible.

The time of fruition can be confusing for those who do not understand the process the Holy Spirit takes to enlightenment—or those who do not want to see what is happening. Little is written about this late stage of the spiritual journey. Fruition can create holy havoc for a time, especially if the process goes unrecognized for what it is, or is pathologized. Fruition is very like a wilderness in which the demons of Mara come sailing forth to have their last gasp as they did with Siddhartha.

Although the Indian scriptures make it clear the work of a disciple is to become the Guru by attaining the Guru's state, many yogis and yoginis, especially in the West, take issue with this claim. Likewise, not many are prepared to give up all of the "5 Ms," which are thought to be obstacles to liberation.

Parting with the 5 Ms can be aided by adopting an Ayurvedic diet if one is Hindu, Buddhist, or a student of the Hindu or Buddhist Tantra. Abiding by Kosher law is helpful if one is working with a Jewish rabbi or a teacher of the Kabbalah. Even Western Christians, who are famous for outrageous community luncheons after church on Sundays, are advised to be less willful with regard to the 5 Ms. A good start for learning how to take care during spiritual process can be found in Dr. Gabriel Cousens's text entitled *Spiritual Nutrition: Six Foundations for Spiritual Life and the Awakening of Kundalini.*

The 5 Ms are: *madya*, liquor; *mansa*, meat; *matsya*, fish; *mudra*, grain; and *maithuna,* sexual intercourse. Although some spiritual seekers find it is harder to give up bread than sex, it is helpful to maintain a healthy diet. Disciples who recognize elevated consciousness in themselves no longer live to eat, but eat to live and continue working for the benefit of others. The cessation of desire is about more than sex. For those who grow up in a society obsessed with sex and power, these two issues generally are the most difficult to release. But, desire has many shapes; it can take the form of a hamburger, a degree from Princeton, or the perfect mate.

Above Makora Point, the 5 Ms assume transformed meanings. *Madya* stands for divine nectar, or *amrit; mansa* for control of speech. *Matsya* points to control of the sacred energy through the practice of *pranayama*, and *mudra* for keeping good spiritual company. *Maithuna*, perhaps the most misunderstood of the 5 Ms, represents *samadhi*, or union of individual mind with cosmic consciousness, rather than undisciplined sexual activity.

Since the Holy Spirit comforts, convicts, and ultimately turns disciples into Gurus, whether they claim to be Gurus or not, he or she is vital to the process of liberation, enlightenment, salvation—thus, the significance of a Shaktipat Guru who is "the way" and "the truth" lighting the road to liberation.

Jesus accepted his work as a Shaktipat Guru, but even the thought of living in such a "Shaktified" state is more than many people—Hindu, Buddhist, Jewish, and Christian—are able to entertain. While difficult to negotiate for many, the time of fruition is a necessary part of the spiritual journey leading to completion of one's spiritual work on planet earth. The time of fruition represents the crossing into freedom.

CHAPTER VIII

Shaktipat by Touch

As a Shaktipat Guru, how did Jesus bestow the precious gift?

Down to washing the feet of his first apostles, touch appears to have been the Master's primary way of bestowing Shaktipat while he was still on earth. However, he also gave Shaktipat by *sankalpa* (will) across the distance and by infusing his sacred energy into food and wine. The ways in which Jesus gave Shaktipat are consistent with the *modus operandi* of Shaktipat Gurus in other traditions.

A Guru can send a ray of energy to a spiritual seeker through the eyes, touch a seeker, give a seeker a mantra, or set of sacred syllables, or will the Shakti to ignite the Kundalini energy at the base of the spine. In the 1990s, for example, an Indian Jagadguru was said to have given Shaktipat to thousands by *sankalpa* and bestowal of the great redeeming mantra, *Om Namah Shivaya.*

In one summer alone, 40,000 spiritual seekers visited the ashram of an Indian Jagadguru in upstate New York. These spiritual travelers could have taken a cruise or flown to Costa Rica for a week of R&R. Instead, they chose to visit a Jagadguru in an ashram, or sacred space. Coupled with the numbers of seekers who have attended Yogic and Buddhist retreats, Charismatic gatherings and Pentecostal revivals, workshops at Kripalu and Omega, this figure makes an important statement about spiritual hunger in contemporary times.

More esoteric ways of giving Shaktipat exist, but details of these transmissions are usually not made public. The Shakti also can be ignited through breathwork, meditation, dreams, and contact with a Shaktipat Guru, both physically and mentally, as well as on etheric planes.

The means by which Shaktipat is given differ according to the orientation of a spiritual path, that is, whether a path is Left-handed or Right-handed Tantra. Right-handed Tantra, generally, is more contained. Both Right-handed and Left-handed Tantra work with erotic energies to fuel Maha Kundalini Shakti, or the Holy Spirit.

Jesus gave Shaktipat by all the means at his disposal, but especially by touch and *sankalpa.* Perhaps his most commonly employed means of giving Shaktipat was by touch. He seems to have been especially fond of touching the eyes of disciples and seekers. One such bestowal of Shaktipat is described in the tale of the two blind men (Matthew 9:27-34) whose eyes Jesus "opened."

The sacred energy Jesus carried was strong. One woman who had been bleeding for 12 years touched the hem of his garment and received his healing energy. The woman was desperate. Considered to be unclean, she was not allowed in the Temple. When she touched the fringe of Jesus's robe, her bleeding stopped instantly (Matthew 9:20, Mark 5: 25-34). Was she bleeding literally or figuratively? Either way, or both, Shaktipat would have worked to effect a healing in this woman who may have been treated as an outcast at the Temple.

If internal conditions are ripe, seekers can receive Shaktipat simply by being in the presence of a Jagadguru. Crowds sought out Jesus just as they did Bhagawan Nityananda and Chogyam Trungpa Rinpoche. Frequently, people say they want to be in the presence of Jagadgurus for their erudite messages and sermons when, more often than not, they want to experience the energy, or Shakti, these precious beings radiate.

Such is the case with Dr. Paul Muller Ortega, a well

known scholar of Kashmir Shaivism and long time practitioner of Yoga, who founded his own group called Blue Throat Yoga. Although Paul, as he is called by his students, has repeatedly insisted he is not a Shaktipat Guru, the Shakti experienced in his presence is very strong. One woman reports having gone into *samadhi,* or meditative absorption, in a teleconference during which Paul was speaking from California, and she was on the other end of the line on the East Coast.

Since the Holy Spirit is the Enlightener, the effects of awakening range from spontaneous transformation via a Brahma Nadi rising to more gradual awakenings. Perhaps the most dramatic example of Shaktipat recorded in Christianity is in the life of Saul, or Paul, in the book of Acts. On the road to Damascus, Paul experienced a cataclysmic spiritual conversion, a 360 degree turn toward the light. Any time "light" is mentioned, the territory is illumined by the Holy Ghost.

Jesus's energy, or Shakti, knocked Paul to the ground and blinded him temporarily. Jesus was operating at a distance, giving Shaktipat by *sankalpa*, so Paul was unsure at first as to whose voice had reached him. After the incident, Jesus dispatched Ananias, one of 70 initiated apostles, to check on Paul. At the end of his speech to the 70 in Luke 10, Jesus said: "Blessed are the eyes that see what you see for I tell you that many prophets and kings wanted to see what you see but did not see it, and to hear what you hear but did not hear it."

Because of Saul's reputation as a murderer of Christians, Ananias resisted following his Master's instructions. Jesus shared his plan for Saul's role in spreading the good news of the Holy Ghost's power, and Ananias relented. Placing his hands on Saul, Ananias, father of John the Baptist, said, "Brother Saul, the Lord—Jesus, who appeared to you on the road as you were coming here—has sent me so that you may see again and be filled with the Holy Spirit" (Acts 9:17).

A Shaktipat Guru may appear on our paths when we least expect it. Nearly 10 months before I received Shaktipat by formal initiation, I began to feel strong energies circulating in my life. One day at a friend's house in Atlanta, I was literally knocked across the kitchen by a bolt of Shakti. Often, when I went out walking in the neighborhood, I felt as if I might fly—simply lift up out of my body and soar over the tops of the large pine trees towering over Emory University and environs.

In the same southern home, a restored Tudor just off of N. Decatur Rd., I witnessed a friend go into a trance while doing Hatha Yoga. The space usually known as the "third eye" opened in her forehead, and she temporarily went unconscious. Her forehead was bleeding. We called in a physician friend who said nothing was wrong that a little rest wouldn't fix.

In the Christian tradition, the wound in my friend's forehead might be called a *stigmata.* Interestingly, although the first Roman Catholic stigmatic is thought to have been St. Francis of Assisi, about 80 percent of those who have experienced stigmatic openings—and the list is quite long—are women. What happened to my friend is a good example of non-Christian stigmata.

Stigmatic openings may be directly related to intense movement of the Shakti, or the Holy Spirit. Admittedly, the sacred energy has been so strong in me I have sometimes felt she might pull my head off my body. The pressure can be intense, intense enough to puncture the skin.

It may strike some as preposterous to think of a

Shaktipat Guru's energy as having such power. Some may be tempted to write Saul's transformation off as a fanciful story told by the author of Acts who wanted to make sure his chapter was included in the *Holy Bible* rather than hidden with the Gnostic Gospels. However, Saul is not alone in the literature of conversions, nor are dramatic conversion experiences restricted to Biblical times. Dramatic experiences like Saul's are not unusual in the oral history of Shaktipat traditions. I, too, experienced a cataclysmic spiritual conversion in August of 1978.

At one of her lowest points, Elizabeth Gilbert, a 21st century journalist and author of *Eat, Pray, Love*, was crawling on the floor beside her bed in pain so acute it resembled *ennui*, or despair. A voice said, in effect, get up off the floor, Elizabeth. The voice could have emerged from Elizabeth's unconscious mind, or it could have come through by transmission from a Jagadguru since Elizabeth wound up spending time at an ashram near Mumbai, India.

I know a woman who had an experience very like Elizabeth's. She was suffering terribly in the wake of a long-term relationship her partner ended to be with someone else. She and her partner were soul mates, she thought, and she had great difficulty accepting the end of their relationship. She, too, was on her hands and knees on the floor. She was crawling toward her *puja*, or sacred altar, when she heard a voice say, Enough! Normally, she was disinclined to trust such promptings, but the message had a positive effect. It led her to stand up, call a therapist, and start the process of letting go.

Assuredly, the Shakti can manifest in messages. Since the Shakti is the same as the Guru, instructions to disciples are frequently delivered on an internal stream. Or, the Shakti can be infused in food and drink. Two marvelous examples from the life of Jesus come readily to mind.

The famous story of how Jesus multiplied the loaves and fishes to feed the 5,000 who had come to be in his presence (Matthew 14:13-21; Mark 6:31-44; Luke 9:10-17; John 6:5-15) stands as an example par excellence of the Shakti at work. All Jesus had to do was whisper an affirmation, and more than enough food was available for everyone to be fed.

Those present were told to sit on the grass. They were fed ambrosia far sweeter than a common meal. They received the divine nectar of Shaktipat. As a colleague, Sandra *Chamatkara* Simon Mangham, a Roman Catholic who serves as Managing Editor of SACRED FEET, says, they were given "supreme *prasad*." From the Sanskrit, *prasad* translates as a gift that carries blessings. If nurtured properly, the blessings can lead to Paradise, or enlightenment.

The second example of Jesus infusing food and drink with Shakti occurred on the evening now commemorated as Maundy Thursday. Its earliest mention occurs in the First Epistle to the Corinthians, and it is recounted in all four Gospels.

On the night before his crucifixion, Jesus gathered his disciples together in the so-called "upper room." The upper room could have been an actual place—maybe on Mt. Zion just outside the walls of Old Jerusalem or in the vicinity of an Essene community. The upper room could also be a symbol for the higher energy vortexes.

Jesus broke bread and invited his disciples to eat. Take this food in remembrance of me, he said. This is my blood, he added, passing the cup. Jesus was inviting his disciples to the first communion service ever in the religion we now know as Christianity. He was urging them to enter the mystic body and accept responsibility for spreading the sacred energy to other beings in the world.

According to Russill Paul, Jesus invited his followers to a "banquet" (*Jesus in the Lotus*, 196), a term employed by Tibetan Buddhists and Sufis as well. The "banquet" is ongoing so long as spiritual practitioners across traditions continue to drink from the "living water," otherwise known as the sacred power of the Holy Spirit.

As Rev. Deefholts mentions in her Introduction to *Jesus Was a Shaktipat Guru,* Christians sometimes do not know about Apostolic Succession as a primary means by which the Holy Spirit is transmitted. Through the great, golden chain leading back to Jesus, apostles through the ages have acted as carriers of the divine nectar.

How unfortunate it is when mainstream Christian churches do not make Apostolic Succession clear. Some do not even mention it. People are told to come and partake of the body and blood of Christ, but often they are not told about the power of the Eucharist to ignite the sacred energy. In the Roman Catholic tradition, of course, there is no difference between the wafer and wine and the body and blood of Christ Jesus. The Eucharist in Catholicism is *chaitanya*, a gorgeous Sanskrit word which means to be embodied by the living power of the Master.

If a Christian minister is clear in his or her intentions, and some assuredly are, the Shakti can also ride the words of a sermon much as Windhorse does during a Buddhist teacher's dharma talk. Listening to a recording of a Guru's words can ignite the holy fire. Chanting, or listening to a chant lead by a Jagadguru, can rouse the sacred energy to holiness beyond compare.

It can be no accident that communion is the most

powerful ritual in Christianity. Baptism is important, too, for its power to wash away impurities. To take the Master's living breath into our bodies is to invite him to guide the Holy Spirit to completion. Such an invitation is comparable to "imbibing the Guru" in the Tantric traditions. When a Jagadguru's energy enters the human system, "even the mystery which hath been hid from ages and for generations" (Colossians 1:26) is made manifest not only to "the saints" but to you and me and anyone who opens to receive.

The most radical claim about Jesus's knowledge of the Holy Spirit is, perhaps, the most doctrinally Christian and the most heretical. Jesus was a saint, a Maha Siddha, who communed with other saints. It is written thusly in "The Apostles' Creed."

How, more specifically, do saints commune? Since Siddhas from all spiritual traditions are omniscient—thus live in Intra-Tantric ethereal dimensions—they need no telephone or computer to dialogue with each other or with their disciples. They commune by transmission and vibration. They have little use for boundaries or dogmas. Their aim is to set human beings free from the devils, *samskaras*, and habitual patterns which threaten to enslave.

If Jesus, Shaktipat Guru, can be contained under a single spiritual heading, he belongs to the Wisdom Tradition. Popularized by Professor Emeritus Huston Smith and given greater currency by Ken Wilber, Wisdom Tradition is a moniker attributed to the inner core or mystical dimensions of virtually all spiritual traditions. Gaining in usage, Intra-Tantric describes the etheric and vibrational dimensions of a Shaktipat Guru's ministry. Ultimately, however, why settle for applying any one single term to an Interspiritual Master like Jesus? As an Indian

Jagadguru once said, at the highest level, there are no labels.

The trappings, doctrines, and power structures usually associated with institutionalized religion are uninteresting to the Wisdom Tradition, which provides a framework for tapping into the deep well of sacred energy and the movement toward enlightenment. Awakening is the primary concern.

"Awake thou that sleepest," Jesus is quoted as saying in Ephesians 5:14. "Arise from the dead, and Christ shall give thee light."

Christ will light the fire, Jesus said. In other words, the fire will blaze from a larger source than one man living in a human body. The fire was spread from the cosmic Christ through the living apostles who acted as conduits for purified consciousness. In Indian terms, the Maha Shakti will ignite the fire moving through the Guru, or teacher who has accepted the responsibility to act on behalf of his or her lineage.

The command from Ephesians could only have been spoken by a Shaktipat Guru who was capable of dispensing the sacred fire—whether by look, touch, or *sankalpa*—which leads unfailingly to freedom.

CHAPTER IX

Jesus, Jewish Shaktipat Guru

Jesus the Christ may have visited India and Tibet. This possibility continues to attract many Westerners, especially those who take issue with the Christian tradition, or those who wish to disassociate Jesus from his Jewish roots.

Jesus may have studied with Yogis high in the Himalayas, or in south Indian caves. It is fascinating to consider the possibilities, but as the Buddhists caution, it is wise to refrain from over-speculation, or invest too much in stories about a great being's life.

Speculations can lead to narratives which have little grounding in reality. When stories overtake the mind, they can blind or create impressions which are then reproduced as fact.

It is, in fact, possible that Jesus learned about the Holy Spirit from the Jewish tradition into which he was born. The first five books of the Old Testament, or the *Torah*, supposedly revealed to Moses at Mt. Sinai, mentions the Holy Spirit more than once as Ruach Hakodesh, breath of God.

Further in the Old Testament, in Isaiah 32:13-18, the Holy Spirit is associated with culmination of the time of fruition, or a "fruitful field:"

> . . . until the Spirit be poured upon us from on high, and the wilderness be a fruitful yield, and the fruitful field be counted for a forest. Then judgment shall dwell in the wilderness, and righteousness remain in a fruitful field and the work of righteousness shall be peace, and the

> effect of righteousness, quietness and assurance forever.

Such passages from the Old Testament can be read as a rabbi promoting piety, but more than likely, the writer was interested in connecting the importance of ethics to spiritual yield. That the Holy Spirit could transform a "wilderness" into a "fruitful field" tends to be lost if too much emphasis is placed on the law or being good to the exclusion of being happy. A detached and balanced analysis finds Jesus emerging from the "wilderness" fruitfully endowed with the gifts of the Holy Spirit and ready to ignite them in others. Quite possibly, if we engage in a literary reading of this passage from Isaiah, the wilderness was internal. Geographically, it likely was located somewhere in the Middle East where the dominant religion was Judaism.

Usually, in Christian circles, Moses is remembered in the Old Testament for scaling a mountain and descending with The 10 Commandments inscribed on a stone. Rarely is Moses associated with the Holy Spirit. Nonetheless, in II Numbers 1:29, Moses was quoted as saying, "Would God that all the Lord's people were prophets and that the Lord would put his Spirit upon them."

Were it, indeed, that the Good Lord would hear Moses's prayer for compassion and put his Spirit upon all humans who remain sleeping. Peace, quietness, and assurance are devoutly to be hoped for in postmodern times when anxiety, noise, and uncertainty are rampant. As more than one modernist writer has said, "People are not evildoers. They are sleepwalkers."

According to Arno Gaebelein, "We may call the Gospel of John, written some time after the Synoptics, the bridge which leads from Judaism to Christianity." In other words, law yields to love as the Holy Spirit works through Jesus to seal the promise of redemption—of fruition.

Gaebelein's 1928 text is rich in knowledge about the Holy Spirit. Gaebelein tracks down virtually every reference to the Spirit in the Christian Bible. For such exhaustive work, he deserves to be celebrated. However, Gaebelein devotes only one paragraph to the verses in Matthew, one of three Synoptic Gospels, in which Jesus calls blaspheming against the Holy Spirit the one unforgivable sin.

According to Matthew 12: 31-32, ignoring the Holy Ghost is the one irredeemable act. Without the Holy Ghost active in our lives, there is little movement toward salvation. We remain stuck in the mire of desire, imagining the projections we flash onto our mental screens to be the truth not only for ourselves, but also for other human beings we involve in our dramas.

How could such a thorough scholar as Gaebelein have given this crucial teaching short shrift? Furthermore, why has the Holy Spirit been swept under the theological rug in much of mainstream Christianity?

Historically, the Holy Spirit carried over from Judaism into Christianity and was integrated into Jesus the Son. Given the dire conditions of the postmodern world in *Kali Yuga*, it may be useful at this point in time to let the Holy Spirit stand on her own sacred feet as Shekinah or Maha Kundalini Shakti, the Holy Ghost in her feminine form. She may be able to travel faster and reach more sleeping souls if she is recognized fully as the magnificent energy which leads to enlightenment rather than being folded into the two masculine figures of God the Father and Jesus the Son.

Jesus was Jewish, and he most likely learned about the Holy Spirit from teachers in his own land. That would not have prevented him from studying in India or Tibet. Study in the countries well known for their systematic attention to the sacred energy would only have strengthened his knowledge as well as his determination to serve humanity by offering Shaktipat.

Across the years, emphasis has been placed on the historical Jesus as well as the political Jesus. Scholars have theorized his life, motives, and whereabouts. Jesus and his teachings have been scrutinized almost as much as *The Bhagavad Gita*—said to be the most "inked" text in religious history—maybe more. An institution has grown up around him, constructed on a foundation of doctrine, dogma, and devotion. Schisms have split the banquet table, and some of Jesus's followers have elected not to break bread with others over matters large and small.

As we head further into the 21st century, "We should never forget that Jesus was essentially a Jewish mystic," as Russill Paul notes in *Jesus in the Lotus* (46). To Russill Paul's incisive comment, I would add: We should never forget that Jesus was primarily a Shaktipat Guru.

When I was on retreat at Shantivanam, the south Indian ashram in which Russill Paul took monastic vows while Father Bede Griffiths was still in his body, I was struck by the Interspiritual architecture and liturgy. Nowhere else in the world had I seen Christian and Hindu traditions fused so beautifully.

Although Father Bede is no longer with us on earth, and Russill Paul has departed the Benedictine order for marriage and life in the world, the power of Jesus's sacred energy remains as vital now as it was when the venerable Bede first arrived in India. No matter the institutional squabbles or political differences, the strength of any tradition depends on its Master Teacher's embodiment of the sacred power and ability to pass the energy on to others—especially when the Teacher is no longer here in the form.

When Jesus had finished washing his disciples' feet, he asked them, "Do you understand what I have done for you?" (John 13:12)

"You call me 'Teacher,' and 'Lord,' and rightly so," he added, "for that is what I am." (John 13:13)

"Now that I, your Lord and Teacher, have washed your feet, you also should wash one another's feet," Jesus continued. (John 13:14)

"Very truly I tell you," Jesus said, "no servant is greater than his Master." (John 13:16)

Do you understand what Jesus did for his disciples? Of course, you do. You have read *Jesus Was a Shaktipat Guru* almost to completion, and you are no longer in the dark as to the power of the Holy Spirit. I understand now, too, but once was the time when I struggled.

When I was little, I spent a lot of time with my grandmother and pop at Slate Branch Farm. I loved playing with the puppies and kitties and making tiny field mice my friends.

"Sonnie, you must believe on the feet of Jesus," my grandmother said. She told me more than once. She did not want me to forget.

"But, Grandmother," I replied, "I don't know how to believe on the feet of Jesus."

It took me 12 years of study and practice in close proximity to an Indian Shaktipat Guru to discover what my deeply Christian grandmother meant. The feet of Shaktipat Gurus are sacred. Their feet contain the Shakti. Their sandals are sacred, too. To believe on the feet of a Shaktipat Guru is to empower one's own sacred feet with the willingness to walk steadily in the direction of liberation, or Christ consciousness.

We hear a lot these days about Christianity as a dying religion. I, for one, must question these doomsday claims. Christianity is still the largest religion in the world, and like other faith traditions, it has been in the process of jumping continents. Who knows, a century from now, what the face of Christianity will look like or where its strongholds will be? For all we know, the "new Jerusalem" may be located in Africa or Australia.

At its core, there is nothing wrong with Christianity, because there is nothing wrong with its Master Teacher. Jesus the Christ is a glorious Jagadguru, deserving of praise down through the ages. In certain sects, however, Christianity has turned its back on the Holy Spirit. Certain of these sects are experiencing sagging vitality and declining membership. Now is not the time for these churches to take their congregations bowling or look for yet another social activity to distract members from the lack of energy in Sunday services. Now is the time to welcome the Holy Spirit back into the heart of Christianity.

In writing this very text, I have re-discovered the profound connection between Jesus and the Holy Ghost. Seeing Jesus through the lens of other Jagadgurus, particularly in Asian traditions, has helped me to recognize Jesus and the Holy Spirit as one. Despite talk of the Trinity, this truth is often hidden in mainstream Christian churches. It needs to be brought forward and articulated clearly. Christians need to be taught how to work with the Holy Spirit in systematic ways much as Yogis are taught how to work with Maha Kundalini Shakti.

When I was about three years old, I went looking for the Holy Spirit at Friendship Methodist Church in the eastern end of Pulaski County, Kentucky.

Friendship was my mother's home church as a girl. She used to walk there for Sunday services from the white clapboard house where she lived with her family. Her father ran a country store and post office just up the road from Sears School, named for Mother's family as both she and her mother taught there. As legend went, Poppy Sears helped a lot of farmers survive the Great Depression.

The preacher was on his knees beside the pulpit. Mary Sue was in her seat on the front pew. When the preacher got excited, Mary Sue did, too. She was wearing orange pop beads, and she sang at the top of her lungs. Something was going on. It was warm inside Friendship Church.

With Mother's eyes closed in prayer, I slid out of our pew and toddled down the aisle. I was wearing a little white crocheted dress Mother had ironed and starched by hand. She always wanted me to look neat and clean.

The preacher opened one eye to see who had decided to pay him a visit during morning prayer. There I stood, staring at him, red hair curly, blue eyes shining. Already a curious theologian, I wanted to know what he was doing down on his knees. I wanted to know why Mary Sue acted different inside the church house than she did at dinners on the ground. I wanted to know why this church felt friendlier than bigger churches where people spent a lot of time standing up and sitting back down.

Before he could open the other eye, a hand reached out for me. Mother had noticed her cherub was missing. She came to retrieve me. She was never one to make a fuss or cause another being any trouble.

I never got around to visiting Mary Sue. Years later, however, I think I know why she sang so loud. The Holy

Ghost got into those pop beads in much the same way Maha Kundalini Shakti gets into the rudraksha beads of Yogis. A string of beads comes alive when Windhorse goes a-flying.

Whether in Dykes, Kentucky, or Trichy, south India, the living power of Christ consciousness prevails. The sacred energy continues to be passed on by apostles representing the different faith traditions. They may be monks well-versed in the scriptures; they may be country preachers who never saw the inside of a seminary; they may be house wives or husbands who like to sing and make a joyful noise to the Lord. Those who are called to serve the Holy Spirit must surely know somewhere inside: essentially, there is only one energy; ultimately, only one Jagadguru with many faces.

After all, the good ole' Christian revival may not be that different in intent from the Shaktipat Intensive. The Vajrayana Buddhist Retreat may not be that far removed from the mystical Jewish group meeting in Dr. Steinbaum's den to ignite the Sephiroth. As Charles Wesley wrote in a hymn entitled "O Thou Who This Mysterious Bread," collected in *The United Methodist Hymnal* (613), the Holy Spirit's work is to "Enkindle now the heavenly zeal."

Jaya Jaya Amrita Guru, praises are due to all the Shaktipat Gurus who have set the Holy Spirit free to do her liberating work—especially Jesus the Christ. *Jaya Jaya Christaya. Jaya Jaya Amrita Guru. Jaya Shri Jagadguru Namah.*

Notes

Apostle's Creed has been spoken in Christian churches during Sunday services across the ages. One woman enrolled in an OSHER class on the Holy Spirit taught by Dr. Jones aka Sw. Shraddhananda and hosted at the Lexington, KY Shambhala Center said she had spoken the words in the creed many times. However, she did not actually understand their meaning until she learned more from Dr. Jones's lectures about the workings of the Holy Spirit as a living power. Likewise, the "communion of saints" takes on new meaning when we become aware of *Ajna* chakra as a subtle body center through which Shaktipat Gurus can communicate with their disciples and with each other.

Arati, or *Sadguru Ki Arati*, is a prayer of nine verses usually chanted in the early mornings and late afternoons.

Brahmacharya, historically, is the first stage of Hindu life as outlined in the *Manusmrti.* Young Hindus undergo a ceremony, and the *brahmacharya* phase usually lasts from 14 to 25 years. Sometimes, non-Hindus under the tutelage of Indian Gurus take the *brahmacharya* vow prior to becoming *sannyasins,* or monks. A new category of *brahmacharya* has emerged with the importation of Eastern religions into the West whereby spiritual seekers take the *brahmacharya* vow later in life as a way to detach from desire. Sometimes, these renunciates go on to become monastics, but not always. Some have been known to marry after spending years as *brahmacharini* living inside the contained space of an ashram. And, sometimes, *brahmacharya* is practiced by married couples as a way to regulate or discipline sexual behavior into a conscious practice. While the equation of *brahmacharya* to asceticism may hold true historically, it is questionable with regard to Western celibates who retain connections to the world and are as comfortable dining in Manhattan as chanting "The Guru Gita." Retention of erotic energy through the practice of *brahmacharya* is distinctly Tantric and is thought to improve focus for meditation and other spiritual practices as well as to enhance the Kundalini's pathways to *ananda*, or ultimate happiness, which arises unconnected to people or events outside itself.

Disciple's Grace is the counterpart to Guru's Grace. Grace, or *kripa,* is a two-way street. Without Disciple's Grace in the form of receptiveness, willingness, and obedience, a spiritual seeker cannot get very far on the journey to liberation. If Disciple's Grace is allowed to diminish, disciples can fall into a stupor.

Dr. Richard Alpert, AKA Ram Dass, author of the now classic text, *Remember, Be Here Now*, is for many Western seekers a major teacher of Indian-based philosophy and practice. When Ram Dass thought he was facing death, he reportedly experienced a moment of self-centeredness, rather than transcendence, which he found to be troubling. This experience is recorded in a 93-minute documentary film directed by Mickey Lemie.

Heaven is not an unusual concept in the world's religions. Some people who were born into Christianity turn away from the faith because of the emphasis some sects place on the afterlife to the exclusion of life on earth. There are other ways of understanding the place where streets allegedly are made of gold. Heaven can be seen as a metaphor for enlightenment. In Hinduism, places after death are known as *lokas*, and in Buddhism, as *bardos*.

Jagadguru, from *Jagat* and *Guru*, literally means, "A Supreme Master of the Entire World." In the *Mahabharata*, from which the *Bhagavad Gita* is excerpted, Arjuna addresses Krishna as a Jagadguru as does the Sanskrit poet Kalidasa use the term for Shiva.

Kali Yuga is the time period in which we now live. It is a very dark time named for the fierce goddess, Kali. According to the *Puranas*, we are about 25,000 years into *Kali Yuga*. Indians divide time periods into large segments called *yugas* which last thousands of years. *Yugas* reflect the vastness of the Indian imagination.

Reincarnation in Christianity swirls around the so-called "Origen controversy" and writings by Christians from 250-553 CE, beginning about 50 years after the death of Origen. In the 6th century CE, Origen Adamantius of Alexandria was a Christian whose ideas were celebrated by some and reviled by others, largely for Origen Adamantius's belief in the pre-existence and rebirth of souls. His work has been rehabilitated by 20th century theologians, Henri de Lubac, SJ and Jean Danielou, SJ.

Rudra Granthi is one of the three knots in the Chakra system. It is the most difficult for Kundalini to penetrate. According to the *Kundalini Tantra*, disciples need not be concerned about Maha Kundalini Shakti climbing into the *Sahasrara*, or seventh chakra, after she has penetrated the brow chakra at *Ajna.* She will naturally stabilize in the *Sahasrara* in time.

Samsara or *sangsara* usually translates from Sanskrit and Pali as "continuous movement" or "continuous flow" through birth, death, and reincarnation. In the West, the term sometimes means the collection of *samskaras,* or embedded karmic imprints, which a seeker must address as he or she moves toward freedom from their effects, sometimes oceanic in their impact. *Samskaras* can lead seekers "to do the same things over and over again, expecting something different to happen," language frequently used by alcoholics in recovery.

Shaktipat experiences fill the oral history of Sacred Feet Yoga, Shiva Yoga, Siddha Yoga and Sikh groups in which the Kundalini energy is active. Manifestations of the Shakti are also common among people involved in Charismatic and Pentecostal groups. While Buddhists do not speak openly of experiences with the sacred energy, practitioners exhibit signs of the sacred energy's movement. One woman reports having attended a teaching in New York City with His Holiness the Dalai Lama during which time the energy became so strong that she could not keep her head still. At one point, she looked up, and His Holiness was staring directly at her, as if to say, "Not here, not now."

Smicha or *semicha* (pronounced Smee-ha), in the time of Jesus, was an ordained rabbi thought to have authority based on special insights into the scriptures. According to Rev. Allen Brimer, Pastor of First Presbyterian Church in Somerset, KY, and founder of the Christian-Muslim Dialogue Group, Jesus could have taken on the role of *smicha* "after graduation" from a training school conducted by his *smicha.* Rather than limiting his teachings to the best students, according to Rev. Brimer, Jesus took the average C students working in fishing boats with their fathers. In this respect, Jesus resembles the Indian Jagadgurus who offered Shaktipat to people regardless of their level of education and knowledge of religious matters.

St. Thomas Aquinas (1225-1274 CE) is one of 33 Doctors of the Roman Catholic Church. He is considered by many to be the Roman Church's greatest theologian and philosopher, his *Summa Theologica,* a classic in philosophical theology.

Synesius's comment about never being thrust back into the world of illusion invokes *mahasamadhi*, a Sanskrit term for the Hindu-Yogic release from the wheel of existence which is sometimes translated as the "great sleep." When great beings take *mahasamadhi*, they merge back into the universe, but because their energy is so powerful, they are still available to people living on earth. Although Christians who are waiting for Jesus to return to earth probably would disagree, it can be said that Jesus took *mahasamadhi.*

Tantra, whether Right-handed or Left-handed, has been a loaded word in the West since the 1960s when it came to be equated in the popular imagination with sex. While *Tantra* certainly works with erotic energies, it cannot be reduced to sex. The question arises: did Jesus practice Right-handed or Left-handed Tantra? So far as we know, Jesus was a Right-handed *tantrika.* Much about his life remains unknown, however, so additional information could overturn virtually any theory postulated about the life and teachings of Jesus.

In early 21st century North America, some very good teachers of the Indian *Tantra* have emerged, among them, Dr. Douglas Brooks, Sally Kempton (formerly Swami Durgananda), and Dr. Paul Muller Ortega. In 2011, Sw. Shraddhananda, then known primarily as Dr. Sonya Jones, introduced Adishraddha, or Sacred Feet Yoga, an Intra-Tantric path which seeks to integrate teachings primarily from the mystical wings of all the world's religions. Sw. Shraddhananda aka Dr. Jones received "The Five Teachings" for Sacred Feet Yoga from June 24 to July 5, 2010, by a process known as transmission. The Tibetan Buddhists might call this process *terma* in that "The Five Teachings" may have been hidden until the time was ripe for a Tantric path with an Interfaith cast to emerge. Literally, *Tantra* means vehicle or weaving. The major scripture associated with the Indian *Tantra* is Abhinavagupta's *Tantraloka.*

Terma teachings are said to be revealed teachings, that is, they are given and arrive unbidden. They are usually associated with the Tantra and can be hidden for a number of years, even centuries, before being revealed. Generally, there are two types of *terma* revealed in objects and in the mind. The Vaishnava saint Chaitanya is thought to have rediscovered a piece of the *Brahma Samhita* while in a devotional trance. It is possible that Moses may have received The Ten Commandments by a process similar to *terma.*

Uriah Heep is an unforgettably cadaverous character from Charles Dickens's novel, *David Copperfield.* Some may regard him as a stereotype, but he appears with some frequency in ashrams and Hatha Yoga studios when obsession with the body overtakes spiritual good sense. Uriah has a fat, stuffy counterpart who likes to turn up his nose at what he perceives as ashram jargon and group-think. Both shrinkers and bloaters meet in "the middle way," known from the time of the Buddha—and the Greek philosopher Aristotle—as a sensible path to undertake.

Windhorse from the Shambhala path brought to the West by Chogyam Trungpa Rinpoche most likely dates back to the shamanic traditions in Tibet prior to the birth of Buddhism. As Windhorse is spoken of in Shambhala training, it may very well be analogous to the Holy Spirit or Maha Kundalini Shakti. Some in the Shambhala tradition might see Windhorse as being closer to good luck or good fortune, but the process of "raising Windhorse" seems to resonate with the Tibetan for vital force, or *srog*, and field of power, or *dbang thang*, which positions Windhorse closer to the illustrious energy we know as the Holy Spirit. Windhorse also derives from the Tibetan *rta chogs* which translates as "the ideal horse with swiftness and wind," surely more powerful than luck. Students in my comparative world religions classes in the West seem to like the idea of Windhorse as a symbol of the sacred energy since the idea of a beautiful horse flying out over the Himalayas is appealing. Some see him as a repository of awakened heart energy, or *bodhichitta.*

Bibliography

Sw. Abhedananda. *Complete Works of Swami Abhedananda.* Ramakrishna Vedanta Math, 1967. Eleven Volumes.

Anadi. *Book of Enlightenment.* http://www.anaditeaching.com

Adyashanti. *Emptiness Dancing.* Sounds True, Inc., 2006.

__________. *The End of Your World: Uncensored Straight Talk on the Nature of Enlightenment.* Sounds True, Inc., 2008.

Dante Alighieri. *The Divine Comedy.* John Ciardi, tr. New American Library, 2003.

Aristotle's Nichomachean Ethics. Robert C. Bartlett and Susan D. Collins, trs. University of Chicago Press, 2011.

Karen Armstrong. *The Great Transformation: The Beginning of Our Religious Traditions.* Anchor, 2007.

Douglas Baker and Celia Hansen. *Super-Consciousness Through Meditation.* Samuel Weiser, Inc., 1978.

Howard Bess. "Was Jesus a Zealot?" http://consortiumnews.com

The Bhagavad-Gita: Krishna's Counsel in Time of War. Barbara Stoller Miller, tr. Bantam Classics, 1986.

Cynthia Bourgeault. *The Wisdom of Jesus: Transforming Heart and Mind—A New Perspective on Christ and His Message.* Shambhala, 2008.

__________. *The Wisdom Way of Knowing: Reclaiming an Ancient Tradition to Awaken the Heart.* Jossey-Bass, 2003.

Malcolm Boyd. *Are You Running with Me, Jesus?* Cowley Publications, 2006. 40th Anniversary Edition.

Gregg Braden. "The 7 Essene Mirrors." http://www.cityofshambhala.net/video/gregg-braden-the-7-essenes

Brad R. Braxton. "The Holy Spirit, Jesus and Social Justice in Black Churches: Making Noise or Making a Difference?" *Huffington Post,* August 23, 2011. http://huffingtonpost.com

Douglas Renfrew Brooks. *Auspicious Wisdom.* State University of New York Press, 1992.

__________. *The Secret of The Three Cities: An Introduction to Hindu Sakta Tantrism.* The University of Chicago Press, 1998.

Rainero Cantalamessa. *Sober Intoxication of the Spirit: Filled with the Fullness of God.* Servant Books, 2005.

Sw. Chidvilasananda (Gurumayi Chidvilasananda). *Courage and Contentment.* Introduction by Stratford Sherman. SYDA Foundation, 1999.

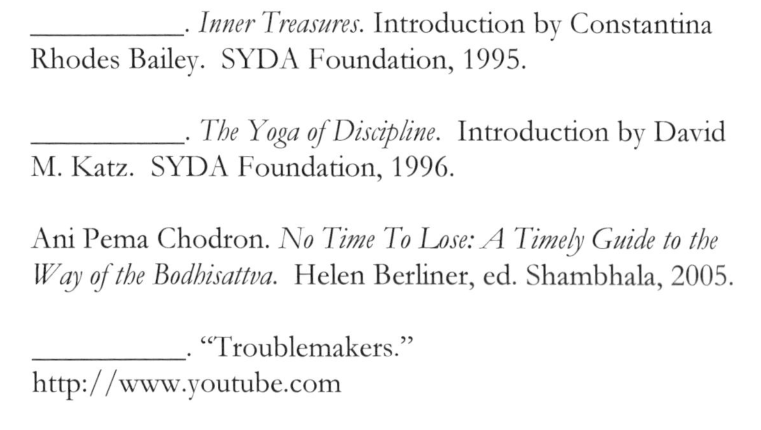

__________. *Inner Treasures.* Introduction by Constantina Rhodes Bailey. SYDA Foundation, 1995.

__________. *The Yoga of Discipline.* Introduction by David M. Katz. SYDA Foundation, 1996.

Ani Pema Chodron. *No Time To Lose: A Timely Guide to the Way of the Bodhisattva.* Helen Berliner, ed. Shambhala, 2005.

__________. "Troublemakers." http://www.youtube.com

Rabbi David A. Cooper. *God Is A Verb: Kabbalah and the Practice of Mystical Judaism.* Riverhead Books, 1998.

Gabriel Cousens. *Spiritual Nutrition: Six Foundations for Spiritual Life and the Awakening of Kundalini.* North Atlantic Books, 2005.

His Holiness the Dalai Lama XIV of Tibet. *Comfort and Ease: The Vision of Enlightenment in the Great Perfection.* Foreword by Sogyal Rinpoche. Wisdom Publications, 2007.

Mary Daly. *Beyond God the Father: Toward a Philosophy of Women's Liberation.* Beacon, Press, 1993. First published by Beacon, 1974.

Dhiravamsa. *The Way of Non-Attachment: The Practice of Insight Meditation.* Turnstone Press, 1984.

Charles Dickens. *David Copperfield.* Serialized, 1849. First published in novel form by Bradbury & Evans, 1850.

John Dickson. *Jesus: A Short Life*. Includes Video Series. Lion Hudson, 2008.

Sw. Durgananda. *The Heart of Meditation*. SYDA Foundation, 2002. Re-published as *Meditation for the Love of It*. Sally Kempton. Sounds True, Inc., 2010.

Mark S.G. Dyczkowski. *The Doctrine of Vibration: An Analysis of the Doctrines and Practices of Kashmir Shaivism*. State University of New York Press, 1987.

Encyclopedia of World Religions. Wendy Doniger and Mircea Eliade, eds. Merriam-Webster and Encyclopaedia Britannica, 1999.

Diana Eck. *A New Religious America*. HarperSanFrancisco, 2002.

Georg Feuerstein. *Tantra: The Path of Ecstasy*. Shambhala, 1998.

Paul Fiddes. "The Theology of the Charismatic Movement." In *Strange Gifts: A Guide to Charismatic Renewal*. David Martin and Peter Mullen, eds. Blackwell, 1984.

Sally Fitzgerald, ed. *The Letters of Flannery O'Connor: The Habit of Being*. Farrar, Sraus, and Giroux, 1979.

Emmet Fox. *The Sermon on the Mount*. HarperOne, 1989. First copyrighted, 1934.

Matthew Fox. *The Coming of the Cosmic Christ*. HarperSanFrancisco, 1988.

E. Franklin Frazier and C. Eric Lincoln. *The Negro Church in America/The Black Church Since Frazier.* Schocken, 1974.
Arno Clemens Gaebelein. "An Exegetical Examination of Every New Testament Reference to the Spirit of God." Publication office "Our Hope." 1928.
http://BibleBelievers.net

"Dr. R.S. Gauer—Kundalini Awakenings"
http://www.youtube.com

Elizabeth Gilbert. *Eat, Pray, Love.* Penguin Books, 2006.

Philip Goldberg. *American Veda.* Foreword by Huston Smith. Harmony Books, 2010.

Edgar J. Goodspeed. *Famous Biblical Hoaxes or Modern Apocrypha.* Baker Book House, 1956.

Elmar R. Gruber and Holger Kersten. *The Original Jesus: The Buddhist Sources of Christianity.* Element Books Ltd., 1996.

Hang Hanegraff. *Counterfeit Revival.* Word Publishing, 2001.

Thich Nhat Hanh. *Living Buddha, Living Christ.* Introduction by Elaine Pagels. Foreword by Brother David Stenindl-Rast. Riverhead Books, 2007.

__________. *You Are Here: Discovering the Magic of the Present Moment.* Shambhala, 2009.

Joan Shivarpita Harrigan. *Kundalini Vidya: The Science of Spiritual Transformation.* Patanjali Kundalini Yoga Care, Sixth Edition, 2005.

Andrew Harvey. *The Direct Path*. Broadway Books, 2000.
M.V. Hatengdi. *Nityananda: The Divine Presence*. Foreword by Sw. Chetanananda. Rudra Press, 1984.

Pete Hayes. *The Supreme Adventure: The Yoga of Perfection*. Foreword by Gurumayi Chidvilasananda. HarperCollins, 1994. First edition published by Delta, 1988.

"Hindu Gurus and Pentecostal Preachers Are Identical."
http://www.bible.ca

"Hindu Tantra—Pancha Makara."
http:/www.yogawiz.com

Holy Bible. King James Version. Thomas Nelson, Inc., 1976.

"Holy Fire."
http://www.youtube.com

"Holy Ghost."
http://www.youtube.com

"Holy Ghost Moving." "Snake Handling." "Whirling Dervishes."
http://www.youtube.com

Quincy Howe, Jr. *Reincarnation for the Christian*. The Theosophical Publishing House, 1987. First edition, Westminster Press, 1974.

J.J. Hurtak. "The Holy Spirit: The Feminine Aspect of the Godhead." The Academy for Future Science, 1993.
http://www.adishakti.org

William James. *The Varieties of Religious Experience*. Classic Books International, 2010.

Kurt Johnson and David Robert Ord. *The Coming Interspiritual Age*. Namaste, 2012.

Sonya Jones aka Sw. Shraddhananda. "A Feminist Reading of the Life and Work of Gurumayi Chidvilasananda." The American Academy of Religion, Chicago, 2002.

__________. "Blue Throat Yoga Teachings with Dr. Paul Muller Ortega Collected Between the Years of 2009 and 2013." Papers held by The Jones Educational Foundation, Inc.

__________. "Cobra, Windhorse, Tree of Light, Dove: The Sacred Energy Across Religious Tradition." Shiva Symposium Series, Shiva Yoga School of Yoga and Meditation, Mt. Eliza, Australia, Aug. 4, 2013; Graymoor Franciscan Retreat, Garrison, NY, for The New Seminary, Sept. 9, 2013; The Big I Conference, Nashville, TN, February 2013.
http://www.jonesfoundation.org

__________. "Commentary on *The Splendor of Recognition* by Sw. Shantananda with Peggy Bendet." *The International Journal of Hindu Studies*, 2007.

__________. "Shambhala Buddhist Teachings Collected Between the Years of 2001 and 2011." Papers held by The Jones Educational Foundation, Inc.

__________. "Siddha Yoga Teachings Collected Between the Years of 1988 and 2014." Papers held by The Jones Educational Foundation, Inc.

__________. *Small Claims, Large Encounters* (poems). Brito & Lair, 1995.

__________. "Studies with Sally Kempton Collected Between the Years of 2002 and 2006." Papers held by The Jones Educational Foundation, Inc.

__________. "Sw. Durgananda: From Radical Feminist to Neo-Tantric Monk." The American Academy of Religion, Atlanta, 2002.

Anodea Judith. *Eastern Body, Western Mind: Psychology and the Chakra System as a Path to the Self.* Celestial Arts, 2004.

__________. *The Sevenfold Journey: Reclaiming Mind, Body and Spirit Through the Chakras.* Crossing Press, 1993.

__________. *Wheels of Life: A User's Guide to the Chakra System.* Llewellyn Publications, 1987.

"Julia Roberts talks about Neem Karoli Baba" http://www.youtube.com

Fr. Thomas Keating. *Open Mind, Open Heart.* Continuum, 1986. Twentieth Anniversary Edition, 2006.

Sally Kempton. *Awakening Shakti.* Sounds True, Inc., 2013.

Hoger Kersten. *Jesus Lived In India: His Unknown Life Before and After the Crucifixion.* Penguin, 2001.

Sw. Kripananda. *The Guru's Sandals: Threshold of the Formless.* SYDA Foundation, 1997.

__________. *The Sacred Power: A Seeker's Guide to Kundalini.* SYDA Foundation, 1995.

Gopi Krishna. *The Evolutionary Energy in Man.* Shambhala, 1997. First published in Great Britain by Vincent Stuart & John M. Watkins, Ltd., 1970.

Zachary F. Lansdowne. *The Chakras and Esoteric Healing.* Motilal Banarsidass, 1993. First published by Samuel Weiser, 1986.

Sw. Lakshmanjoo and John Hughes. *Shiva Sutras: The Supreme Awakening.* AuthorHouse, 2007.

Sw. Lakshmanjoo. *Vijnana Bhairava: The Practice of Centering Awareness.* Indica Books, 2007.

C.W. Leadbeater. *The Chakras.* Quest Books, 1997. Copyright 1927 by The Theosophical Publishing House.

Mickey Lemie. "Ram Dass, Fierce Grace." Lemie Pictures, Inc. 2002.

Theodore M. Ludwig. *The Sacred Paths: Understanding the Religions of the World.* Prentice-Hall, Inc., 2001.

Geddes MacGregor. *Reincarnation in Christianity: A New Vision of the Role of Rebirth in Christian Thought.* Quest Books, 1990.

Meditation Revolution: A History and Theology of the Siddha Yoga Lineage. Baily, Brooks, Durgananda, Mahony, Muller Ortega, and Sabharathnam. Agama Press of the Muktabodha Indological Research Institute, 1997.

Fr. Thomas Merton. *The Seven Storey Mountain.* Mariner Books, Anniversary Edition, October 1999.

Marvin W. Meyer and James M. Robinson. *The Nag Hammadi Scriptures: The Revised and Updated Translation of Sacred Gnostic Texts.* HarperOne, 2009.

Baba Muktananda. *Kundalini Stavah.* SYDA Foundation, 1980.

__________. *Play of Consciousness: A Spiritual Autobiography.* Introduction by Gurumayi Chidvilasananda. SYDA Foundation, 2000.

Caroline Myss. *Anatomy of the Spirit: The Seven Stages of Power and Healing.* Harmony, 1997.

Nicolas Notovich. *The Unknown Life of Jesus Christ.* Wilder Publications, 2008.

I.M. Oderberg. "Reincarnation as Taught by Early Christians." *Sunrise* Magazine, Theosophical University Press, May 1973.

Carl Olson. *Indian Philosophies and Postmodern Thinkers: Dialogues on the Margins of Culture.* Oxford University Press, 2002.

__________. *The Different Paths of Buddhism: A Narrative-Historical Introduction.* Rutgers University Press, 2005.

Paul Muller Ortega. *The Triadic Heart of Shiva.* State University of New York Press, 1989.

Elaine Pagels. *The Gnostic Gospels.* Vintage, 1989. First copyrighted, 1979.

Raimon Panikkar. *The Intra-Religious Dialogue.* Paulist Press, 1999.

Patanjali. *The Yoga Sutras.* Swami Satchidananda, tr. Integral Yoga Publications, 1990.

Kassondra Patterson. "Journey along a well-lit path." *Union College Alumni Magazine.* Summer 2011.

Russill Paul. *Jesus in the Lotus: The Mystical Doorway between Christianity and Yogic Spirituality.* New World Library, 2009.

Elizabeth Claire Prophet. *The Lost Years of Jesus: Documentary Evidence of Jesus's 17-Year Journey to the East.* Summit University Press, 1984.

Dwight and Karen Pryor. *Behold the Man.* Center for Judaic-Christian Studies, 2005.

Ram Dass. *Remember, Be Here Now*. Hanuman Foundation, 1971.

__________. *Still Here: Embracing Aging, Changing, and Dying.* Riverhead Books, 2001.

Reginald A. Ray. *Indestructible Truth: The Living Spirituality of Tibetan Buddhism*. Shambhala, 2000.

L.M. Richardson. "Practical Lessons in Christian Mysticism."
http://ww.chrymysticaloutreach.com

Chogyam Trungpa Rinpoche. *The Collected Works*. Carolyn Gimian, ed. Shambhala, 2003.

Sakyong Mipham Rinpoche. *Turning the Mind into an Ally*. Foreword by Pema Chodron. Riverhead Books, 2003.

Sw. Satyananda Saraswati. *Kundalini Tantra*. Bihar School of Yoga, 1996.

Gershom Scholem. *Major Trends in Jewish Mysticism*. Foreword by Robert Alter. Schocken Books, 1995. Based on the Hilda Strook Lectures delivered by Professor Scholem at the Jewish Institute of Religion, New York.

"Scientific Proof of Reincarnation: Dr. Ian Stevenson's Life Work."
http://reluctant-messenger.com/reincarnation-proof.htm

"The Secret Book of James." In Marvin W. Meyer and James M. Robinson. *The Nag Hammadi Scriptures.* HarperOne, 2009.

"Shaktipat Diaries-1-Experience of a New Yorker" http://www.youtube.com

Sw. Shankarananda. *Consciousness Is Everything: The Yoga of Kashmir Shaivism.* Shaktipat Press, 2000.

Sw. Shantananda with Peggy Bendet. *The Splendor of Recognition.* SYDA Foundation, 2003.

Robert Shiarella. *Journey to Joy: An Introductory Guidebook to Siddha Meditation.* Matrika Publications, 1982.

Shunryu Suzuki Roshi. *Zen Mind, Beginner's Mind.* Shambhala, 2011.

Lilian Silburn. *Kundalini: The Energy of the Depths.* Jacques Gontier, tr. State University of New York Press Series in the Shaiva Traditions of Kashmir, 1988. French edition, 1983.

Jaideva Singh. *The Yoga of Delight, Wonder, and Astonishment: A Translation of the Vijnana-bhairava.* Foreword by Paul Muller Ortega. State University of New York Press, 1991.

"The Smile at Fear Teachings." *Shambhala Sun*, March 2011. In Honor of Pema Chodron. Includes Carolyn Gimian, "Discovering the Power of Basic Goodness."

Huston Smith. *The World's Religions.* HarperOne. 50th Anniversary Edition, May 2009.

__________. *Why Religion Matters: The Fate of the Human Spirit in an Age of Disbelief.* HarperSanFrancisco, 2001.

John Stanko. "New Testament Bible Study." http://www.johnstanko.com

David Stern. *Complete Jewish Bible and Jewish New Testament Commentary.* Messianic Jewish Resources International, 2001.

Andrew Strom. *KUNDALINI WARNING—Are False Spirits Invading the Church?* RevivalSchool, 2014.

__________. "The Toronto Controversy." http://www.streetrevival.com

Stefanie Syman. *The Story of Yoga in America.* Farrar, Straus & Giroux, 2009.

Wayne Teasdale. *The Mystic Heart.* Foreword by His Holiness The Dalai Lama. New World Library, 1999.

Sw. Shivom Tirth. *A Guide to Shaktipat.* Devatma Shakti Society, 1985.

Ireena Tweedy. *Daughter of Fire: A Diary of a Spiritual Training with a Sufi Master.* The Golden Sufi Center, 1986 and 2006.

The United Methodist Hymnal. Nashville: The United Methodist Publishing House. 1991.

Llwellyn Vaughan-Lee. *The Face Before I Was Born: A Spiritual Autobiography.* The Golden Sufi Center, 2009. First edition, 1997.

Christopher D. Wallis. *Tantra Illuminated: The Philosophy, History, and Practice of a Timeless Tradition*. Anusara Press, 2012.

Alan Watts. *Behold the Spirit: A Study in the Necessity of Mystical Religion*. Vintage Books, 1972.

Cornel West. *African American Religious Thought*. Westminster John Knox Press, 2003.

Warren W. Wiersbe. *Jesus in the Present Tense: The I Am Statements of Christ*. David C. Cook, 2011.
http://letusreason.org

Ken Wilber. *No Boundary: Eastern and Western Approaches to Personal Growth*. Shambhala, 1979 and 2001.

__________. *The Essential Ken Wilber: An Introductory Reader*. Shambhala, 1998.

Lola Williamson. *Transcendent in America: Hindu Inspired Meditation Movements as New Religion*. New York University Press, 2010.

Alexander Wynne. *The Origin of Buddhist Meditation*. Routledge, 2007.

Lama Yeshe. *The Bliss of Inner Fire: Heart Practice of the Six Yogas of Naropa*. Wisdom Publications, 1998.
Paramahansa Yogananda. *Autobiography of a Yogi*. Self Realization Fellowship, 1998.

__________. *The Second Coming of Christ: The Resurrection of the Christ Within You.* Self-Realization Fellowship, 2004. Two Volumes.

__________. *The Yoga of Jesus: Understanding the Hidden Teachings of the Gospels.* Self-Realization Fellowship, 2007.

About Slate Branch Ashram

Photo by Sandra Simon Mangham

SLATE BRANCH ASHRAM
Home of Adishraddha Yoga
An Interfaith, Interspiritual, Intra-Tantric Path
Devoted to Nurturing the Sacred Energy

"Slate Branch Ashram is a lovely retreat center set in the magnificent rolling hills of rural Kentucky. It's a wonderful place to unwind and receive deep spiritual renewal. Spiritual work at Slate Branch is enhanced by delightfully delicious vegetarian meals enjoyed in warm fellowship with seekers of many different religions and cultural backgrounds."

--Dr. Constantina Rhodes
Author, *Invoking Lakshmi: The Goddess of Wealth in Song and Ceremony*

"I woke up in the night at Slate Branch and could see the sky full of stars. It's so quiet and dark that you can feel yourself being."

--Jane Gentry Vance
Former Poet Laureate of Kentucky

"Slate Branch Ashram and Sw. Shraddhananda are blessings to us all."

--Gloria Garrett
Health and Lifestyle Consultant, ApenGlow Healing Center, LLC

"I really learned a lot at Slate Branch about how I tend to overreact to people and situations. I learned that I can choose not to overreact."

"It was really fun to experience some of the practices at the ashram that we learned about in our seminar on religious plurality in postmodern times."

"I am a Christian, but our seminar and our visit to Slate Branch Ashram has allowed me to see that there is truth and goodness in all the world's religions."

"It's hard not to be stressed as an Honors student at UK. Meditation in our seminar and at the ashram really helped me to be calm."

"My legs hurt at first during meditation, but the more we did it, the better I liked it."

"I was so surprised by Slate Branch—I even liked the chanting!"

"I would like to do more Yoga. It feels so good!"

"I was not raised in any religion, and now that I am learning about them, I think I would like to explore Buddhism in greater depth."

"After my experience at Slate Branch Ashram, I am really looking forward to traveling to India with Dr. Jones and visiting the Hindu temples."

"Learning about the world's religions made me appreciate my own Roman Catholicism even more."

"I must be a Monist. I don't see any difference in any of the world's religions. The bottom line truths are all the same to me. They are all wonderful."

"There's no question—Dr. Jones's teaching has changed my life."

--University of Kentucky Honors Program Students

About the Author

Photo by Melissa Reid

Sw. Shraddhananda aka Rev. Dr. Sonya Jones, OUnI serves as Spiritual Director of Slate Branch Ashram, located in the beautiful Lake Cumberland Valley of Kentucky. She teaches comparative world religions in the Honors Program at the University of Kentucky and for The New Seminary in New York City. A member of the Saraswati Order of Monastics, she holds a Ph.D. from Emory University. She has lectured on six continents.

Jesus Was a Shaktipat Guru
is also a series of lectures on
Wholistika
http://wholistika.com

Made in United States
Orlando, FL
10 August 2023

35950675R10114